DUNLIN PRESS

PORT

Edited by

MW Bewick and Ella Johnston

PORT

Published by Dunlin Press in 2019

Dunlin Press
Wivenhoe, Essex
dunlinpress.com | @dunlinpress

A CIP record of this book is available from the British Library.

ISBN: 978-0-9931259-6-6

Set in Helvetica and Adobe Garamond.
Additional words by MW Bewick and Ella Johnston.
Book illustration and design by Ella Johnston.

Contents

What is a Port?

What is a port? The answer, at first, might seem simple and obvious. A port is a place where ships are loaded and unloaded. But as with many things that at first seem simple and obvious, sense and understanding have a habit of fraying and unravelling, like discarded rope found on an old quay. A port is a harbour or a haven, but what does that mean? Ports are the towns and cities in which the harbours and docks are located. What kinds of town? What kinds of city? Are the ports just the buildings and infrastructure, or the people who live and work there? And are they always large centres of trade? What about the smaller working ports, or the ports where the primary commercial activities have ceased?

A port is a place of arrival, a point for departure, a place where 'here' contacts 'there'; where known and unknown meet; where perceptions of possible experience are expanded. From the traditional fishing village to the mechanised container city, to the old docks redeveloped into marinas and cultural quarters, time shapes our ports and ports shape people and society. Who lives there? What happens there? When and why does the success or failure of a port occur? How do ports frame our experiences? In what kinds of landscapes are they sited? What nature co-exists there? What distant lands do they connect?

There are around 120 commercial ports in the United Kingdom. These range from major all-purpose ports such as London and Liverpool, or specialised and highly mechanised container ports such as Felixstowe, to ferry ports such as Dover, and ports catering for particular types of bulk traffic such as coal or oil. Then there are the smaller fishing ports, some of which hardly land a catch in the 21st century, and the ports that are now reinvented as leisure hubs and lined with pleasure craft.

Around 95 per cent of UK imports and exports are still transported by sea. Much of the volume of freight is handled by the major ports, with the top 20 ports accounting for 88 per cent of the total traffic. According to government figures, in 2018 UK ports handled 483.3 million tonnes of cargo. Imports exceed exports, with a total of 252.4 million tonnes heading into the UK, compared to 130.5 million tonnes leaving these shores. Some 118,000 people are directly employed in UK ports, which also support around 350,000 other jobs. Their contribution to UK GDP is around £19 billion.

Controlling more than 42 per cent of UK's containerised trade, the Port of Felixstowe, in Suffolk, is Britain's biggest and busiest container port, the sixth busiest in Europe, and 35th worldwide. But beyond the commercial and giant cargo-handling ports, there are more than 400 other ports and harbours around the UK, bringing in tourist trade and bonding communities through their history and heritage. In even the most remote of UK locations, a port remains a draw. People come, linger, look, wonder.

In selecting the writing for this anthology, we wanted to cover these extremes, and also survey ports and port life from all around the UK's coastline – and, sometimes, into its interior and beyond. The trade figures can only ever tell a fraction of the story, and that's why the poems and prose you'll find here take a human view of the various locations.

The breadth of writing and experience in this volume is as diverse as the ports themselves. Poet and musician Martin Newell finds a picture of pre-fame John Lennon on a Harwich quay, which leads to a story of wartime Kindertransport. In Tim Cook's reflections on adolescence in Port Talbot, we gain a view of an industrialised coastline from the top of a mountain. Kerri ní Dochartaigh leads us to the "echoing hum of machinery" and the legacy of Irish famine. Mark Ranger takes us to view port landscapes as sites of "exclosure", pocked by cracks and potholes where nature still finds a way – "an eruption of things lain dormant".

We explore places where sugar cane, rum, tobacco and cocoa reached British shores – products of the trade in slaves – and also where John Wesley spoke out against that trade, and where today anti-establishment voices are expressed as street art. With Jason Gould in Hull we find the port as an "instrument of enterprise, symbol of siege", and in Liverpool and Felixstowe with Dr Anna Sergi, an expert in criminology and ports, we trace the "illicit trafficking … that follows the established routes of legal trade".

Poet Golnoush Nour links the UK to a place of personal departure – to the "sealess port / Tehran, the harbour of pollution / the scenario of our eternal escape", while Rebecca Gethin surveys the maritime maps to see how the ships that come to our ports from "the Arabian Gulf sit it out / till the price of oil rises or falls". We hear from artist Matei Bejenaru about Romanian refugees "sneaking into and finding air pockets in shipping containers", and learn about 'The Block' – the solitary confinement units in immigration detention centres.

Sarah Jasmon drives us along the Manchester Ship Canal to find Port Salford, where we discover a "port without a port, without a dock, or a connection to water or even a view of water". Author Chris Maillard points us to the airport, which becomes "a place of possibilities and potential" where people "eradicate the barriers of distance and time". We hear stories of hardship, of the twists and turns of history, which sometimes beats at the ports harder than any ocean wave. And we see people, and nature, refusing to submit, weathering life's storms. As poets Vahni Capildeo and Tessa Berring write: "A port is never over ... A harbour is where voices call back."

The Place of Ships

Njord. Njord. Gulls cough my name,
string-legged on the sea-edge road.

When they are broken
I cup in my hands
their heartsong of falling.

In the morning, still sleepless,
you rolled over to confess
that these seabirds do not sing, they grieve.

So we migrate from place to place
damp with sea-smoke,
clouds tiding your home, up here on the rocks –

if I were to jump from this high place,
my body would run with albumen, glair.

Jessica Mayhew

An Old Essex Seaport

It's only a black and white snapshot of an overloaded Commer van being hoisted by crane onto a ferry. A few port workers are standing, overseeing the job. In the bottom left-hand corner of the picture a young man, his back to the camera, standing idly observing the van with its overloaded roof rack. It's 16th August 1960 and a 19-year-old John

Lennon is about to embark upon the journey that will change his life. When, just over two decades later, he lies dying from gunshot wounds in a New York street, he'll have become one of the most famous people of the 20th century. At this point, however, nobody in Harwich, where this snap was taken, let alone the rest of the world, has yet heard of The Beatles. All from Liverpool, a much larger port in the northwest of England, the band members at present are only a rough-hewn teenage quintet. After a few months in Germany they'll return to Liverpool with the musical muscle of young warriors. Within a few years, culturally, they'll have changed the world. Right now, however, they're at Parkeston Quay Harwich, waiting to take the ferry to the Hook of Holland, en route to a residency in Hamburg.

Harwich, a small seaport on the north Essex coast, has, at the time of writing, a population of just under 18,000. It stands at the confluence of the rivers Orwell and Stour, gazing out across the old German Sea. On the Suffolk side of the estuary, like a flouncier, ringletted sister, sits Felixstowe, a seaside resort popular in late Victorian times.

After sea cargoes were containerised in the 1970s, however, Felixstowe became the UK's biggest container port, far superseding Harwich. A hard-working old town, Harwich never fully recovered from this blow and even now seems to carry upon it a residual air of melancholy. The town though, even during its Maytime, and unlike Felixstowe, was hardly regarded as genteel. Daniel Defoe, in spring of 1722, wrote of his visit: "The inhabitants are far from being famed for good usage to strangers but on the contrary, are blamed for being extravagant in their reckonings in the public houses." He added, however, that "Harwich is a town of hurry and business, not much of gaiety and pleasure, yet the inhabitants seem warm in their nests and some of them are very wealthy." If you want an idea of exactly how wealthy some of residents were in Defoe's time, there are several fine Georgian houses and buildings still to be observed in the Old Town, especially around the area of its quay. The old part of Harwich is beautifully preserved – not in some anodyne History'n'Heritage way but carefully and without the cloying sheen of twee-ness. Other old English towns might do well to learn from it.

For many centuries, Harwich remained the gateway to northern Europe. It was from here that we traded goods and fought wars with the Dutch, the Germans and the Scandinavians – most of our northern European neighbours, in fact. Harwich was pivotal, in times of both trade and of war, its name stamped through British naval history like Blackpool's is through sticks of seaside rock.

The *Mayflower*, which sailed from Plymouth in 1620 with the Pilgrim Fathers aboard, was actually built in Harwich and its captain, Christopher Jones, was from a Harwich family. The old town itself seems to swash around in its own history.

Harwich's salience as a port was evinced by the fact that for many years it fielded two Members for Parliament. In the 17th century, one of the MPs was Samuel Pepys.

Better known by a prurient reading public as a diarist with a fondness for dalliances with his wife's maids, Pepys was actually a senior naval administrator and a founder of our modern Civil Service. A few decades later, another Samuel, Dr Samuel Johnson, came to Harwich to see his young biographer Boswell off on a Grand Tour of Europe.

The town is perhaps too modest about itself. With accounts stretching back to the Anglo-Saxon Chronicles, it possesses more historical riches than many places.

In the 16th and 17th centuries came two separate waves of Huguenot and other religious refugees from Flanders and the Netherlands. Arriving in Harwich, they'd have come down the old Colchester Road in wagons and carts, en route to London. Many others, however, settled in the region, especially in Colchester, giving name to the town's famous Dutch Quarter.

These migrants brought with them weaving and building skills, reviving in the process Colchester's ailing cloth-making trade and adding flavour to the local architectural style. Those distinctive Flemish roofs, for instance, which are actually old Spanish in origin, are still to be seen around north Essex today.

Over the 17th and 18th centuries, the English fought four naval wars with the Dutch. During the second of these, in 1667, the Dutch 'invaded' Harwich with a force of 1,500 marines and 500 sailors. They didn't do very well. The battle lasted only a day or so and they retreated, having lost 150 of their men, to only about ten of ours.

Harwich, to its eternal credit, also served in the months leading up to WW2 as host to the Kindertransport. This was a visionary rescue mission organised by Nicholas Winton, an English-Jewish stockbroker, sometimes dubbed 'the British Schindler'. Under his aegis, approximately 10,000 European Jewish refugee children passed through the port, successfully saved from the Nazi death camps. When, during 2008, the 70th anniversary of the Kindertransport occurred, Harwich councillors were puzzled and somewhat hurt to discover that the town had been by-passed in the more general commemorations in favour of London.

I visited Harwich during this time and was invited by councillors into the Guildhall, a beautiful Georgian building from which council business is run. In the days of the Napoleonic wars, everything was done pretty much in-house at the Guildhall. As well as council business, wrongdoers were tried there and if found guilty, they were gaoled there too, in a chamber now nicknamed the 'Graffiti Room'. When the old wooden walls of the chambers were uncovered a few years ago, the 'graffiti' was found: pictures of old sailing ships immaculately carved into the planks by bored French prisoners of war. A whole wall of it is still there.

If it happened that the jail was full, they'd put the captives in cages outside, or down in the less-than-fragrant cellar. A man was paid a shilling to come once a week and remove the necessary from the crude facilities. It probably wasn't enough money.

Upstairs in the Guildhall, I was shown a simple and highly

moving exhibition, consisting mostly of photographs and letters, commemorating Die Kindertransport. The first few hundred child refugees disembarked in early December of 1938 and were accommodated either in the newly built Warners Holiday Camp or with the Salvation Army. The children arrived at the onset of a hard Essex winter, its chill counter-balanced only by the warmth of their hosts. Letters from a handful of those still alive today attest to this. They have never forgotten the kindness of the Harwich people.

Also in the exhibition were a few Red Cross telegrams from the children's parents, whom in most cases, they would never see again. "Umarmen küssen herzlichst" – "Heartfelt hugs and kisses" – read one. The resolution of some of the photographs is extraordinary. But for the clothing and haircuts, the pictures might have been taken last week. Not that many of the children here look tearful or traumatised. For the older ones it would have been something of an adventure and in some cases you can see it on their faces. The war, let alone the resultant holocaust, had not yet begun, although its shadow was already across the sun. The children were looked after, kitted out and dispersed to foster homes all round the country. All through the build-up to the war in 1939, successive waves arrived, until 10,000 little souls, who would escape the horror of the concentration camps, had passed safely through Harwich. Considering that this exhibition consisted of mere card and paper, it was very potent stuff. It also reminded me that for our manifold faults, the English are a remarkably kindly people, once you dig beneath that infamous reserve of theirs. Harwich as we see, is great not just for what it has and that which we can see, but surely for what has passed through the place on the way to sanctuary – or to greatness.

We return to the snapshot of John Lennon on the Harwich quayside in August 1960. At this time the five Beatles: John Lennon (19), Paul McCartney (18), Pete Best (19), Stuart Sutcliffe (20), and George Harrison (17), were at best a shambolic, semi-pro pop group who'd only recently graduated from coffee bars to playing dance halls. Weeks earlier, Alan Williams, their manager, had signed a contract for four months' work in Hamburg. With hastily arranged passports and work permits, off they went. After disembarking in Holland, the band headed north to Hamburg, a place that the wide-eyed young Harrison, yet to lose his virginity, described as 'the naughtiest city in the world'.

Thus, a mere 15 years after the end of World War II, did the raw young scousers begin a job of work that would last until almost the end of November. In the seamy Indra club and later, the Kaiserkeller, they'd play an exhausting five or six sets per night, propped up by beer and Preludin – amphetamine-like appetite suppressant pills they acquired semi-legally. Their billet was an ill-lit squalid room behind the screen at the Bambi Kino cinema. They lived on bowls of cornflakes and café food and were befriended by the waiters, bouncers and prostitutes who also worked in the clubs. Pilled-up, half-cut and worked like dogs, Hamburg got The

Beatles well and truly into harness. Upon their return to Liverpool, vulcanised by the experience, they must have hit their hometown like a ton of flying bricks.

That first Hamburg stint, however, ended in ignominy. Three months into their residency, a rival club owner made a pitch for them. The club owner with whom they were contracted was furious. In late November, the Hamburg police descended, stating that George Harrison, at 17 years of age, was too young to be working. He was deported. I have often wondered how he got home. After some rooting around, I stumbled upon George's own account.

"Astrid and probably Stuart dropped me at Hamburg station. It was a long journey on my own on the train to the Hook of Holland. From there I got the day boat. It seemed to take ages and I didn't have much money – I was praying I'd have enough. I had to get from Harwich to Liverpool Street Station and then a taxi across to Euston. From there I got a train to Liverpool. I can remember it now: I had an amplifier that I'd bought in Hamburg and a crappy suitcase and things in boxes, paper bags with my clothes in, and a guitar. I had too many things to carry and was standing in the corridor of the train with my belongings around me, and lots of soldiers on the train, drinking. I finally got to Liverpool and took a taxi home – I just about made it. I got home penniless. It took everything I had to get me back."

Just over a week later, Paul McCartney and Pete Best were arrested on a spurious charge of attempted arson. They too were deported. The authorities put the pair of them on a flight to London, from where they managed somehow, to get back to Liverpool with the last of their money. Stuart Sutcliffe, the bass player, stayed on in Hamburg, hiding out at his German girlfriend Astrid's house. Finally, in early December, John Lennon, lonely and homesick, also left Hamburg, coming home to Liverpool by rail and ferry. For some time after their return there was no contact between the band members. Paul McCartney even briefly took a job in a local factory. This tail-between-legs situation didn't last long, however. The band soon regrouped, this time as a quartet, without Stuart Sutcliffe. They were gigging again by mid-December. Hamburg had improved them beyond belief. It's often been recounted that within minutes of them taking the stage, people, magnetised by the spectacle, would flock to the front. It was the birth of Beatlemania.

In April 1961, after some telephone diplomacy and a few cleared slates, The Beatles returned to Hamburg for second similarly gruelling three-month stint – this time to a better club and rather better wages. They came through Harwich again, returning the same way the following July. This, however, was the last time that Harwich would see them. Their star was already rising as their youthful anonymity was disappearing. Subsequent trips to Hamburg would all be undertaken by plane. As I stood in Harwich recently, gazing across the water, it occurred to me once again, that The Beatles had passed through here on their way to glory.

And one day, in late November of 1960, a disconsolate

17-year-old George Harrison came trailing through once again, lugging his guitar, his amp and his tatty luggage. The train from Parkeston Quay would have taken him past Dovercourt and Manningtree, through Colchester and on to London. Then, after a taxi to Euston, another long train ride home to his mum's house in Liverpool. Little could he have guessed what awaited him in the next chapter. If I were a Harwich councillor, I'd have a plaque put up, saying, "In August 1960, The Beatles left for Hamburg from here." Because that's what happened.

Martin Newell

Crossing The Minch

still   the wind cannot raise a flag

still   the sky wears a thin blue glaze
cracking at the edges

still   there is no rush to kiss white peaks
onto the endless mountain ranges of the sea

still   Assynt   An Teallach and the Quiraing
present a rugged countenance of farewell

still   the boat persists over the corkscrew
currents of the wine-dark water

still   to tundral Stornaway   wind-blasted
and rock-hugging   like lichen   yet still

Nick Allen

Shapeshifter Haven

Anchors are stuck in the street. How heavy they are. How solemn. The depths they have been plunged into, dragged back from. The cross-street inlets run dry except in Icelandic memories of Scotland. Imagine cold: ice, everything melting, frozen stars, birds, boats. This east coast port was a place of repair, as well known as Shetland, though less mapped. There are no willows where the sign names willows. What is willows? asks someone. What is inlets? What is salt? Children climb the black-painted anchor tree.

Children clamber into hot baths of lavender foam. Lucky they are. And a blue towel on the radiator. They must brush their teeth. Ice cream and fish, ice cream and fish. Singing, and the steam lessens as the bath cools. Outside is dark. The anchor means every anchor. A sign says, what does it say? Look closer in the morning. Rivulets of breath water the air. The bus runs along slopes reclaimed from sea. Passengers offer exact change. Zero seems warm. O like an open mouth, O like a bubble. Zero is the stillest number, Nothing, just an edge.

The buses are full of people breathing, waiting for the right time to leave. But some things are not close enough, others not far enough away. Here is an ice swan on a long table! Where did it come from? Cousin, perhaps, to the sugar swan in a former Spanish port, its feathery back a tumble of yellow birthday-icing tea-roses? O the redness in the sky, pink as a sore eye. Graffiti by the old mills, turquoise as chlorinated water.

Blink, O sea. The sea blinks like always; the port winks like always. Is this my ship? Always children to put to sleep, always singing. Always staircases spiralled into walls, one for the fish storage floor, another for the attic. Always living rooms, always kitchens, windows open or closed. The air washes in, then out, hauling scents: aubergine and juniper, salt crystals, tobacco and ground flour. And think of the sand dunes, O, won't you.

Warmth: the impulse to unstick things? Warmth: the port being less shadow than colour? What map? O is tired of being poised. Of being closed. 'O rivers,' thinks O. The weight of walls, the fragility of telescopes, finger-holds worn into stone by women of similar height, coming and going in their shoes and on their tiptoes, imagining duels on staircases spiralled into walls.

O, what hides in a fisher's attic, or in the choir of flowers at the red door? Pink and purple illuminations, soundless fireworks over water named Water, galaxies inside eyelids, the clash of swords in a narrow space? The body of O. A decommissioned lighthouse that the children long to climb. A port: where you are when you do, don't, have to go anywhere. A port: where there is going.

Land ahoy! Flowers with names like feverfew and vetch. Here love, people are yawning in the café on the horizon. The moon goes up and down too. The way things sink behind lines, or sail across them. Different spaces fit like fish tabled for sale on a fishwife's forearm, head to tail, wrist to elbow. Who counsels the council? Who skewers the eels? The fishwives have been forbidden the buses. Scent away. Salt can't commute. Cockles once were called cockles, soft in a hard dark O. The passengers riverrun a cleansed track. The sailor on leave is restless with enjoyment. Here. Oh, you are good at this, says the enjoyment, says the leaving, says the empty bus on the shore.

Morning is closer. What does the sign say? 'Morning,' says the sign, or seems to. The cobbles click with low heels and walking sticks. These strange, cold, silver girls disdain overcoats as if they were in Bombay on loungers, the Arabian sea at their backs, not under the thin uprights of leafless bird cherry trees. Ice melted off another sign; a sign without words, like a song written for piano and no voice. Something for touching, for looking at, for moving off… Picture writing. Casting off. Ghosts.

The greatest density per square centimetre of ghost anywhere in the world is pinpointable to one street in the Old Town. Dense ghosts are compacted inland. Ghosts in view of a horizon stay fresh for longer. The ghost with a name nobody can pronounce; it rhymes with the sound of sugar. Did the anchor spin like a weathercock arrow? Did the sun blink behind the lining clouds?

The sign points to land reclaimed from the sea, now a channel of tarmac, and says water. The sign points to the water called Water, and says nothing. The children find Your Location on an electronic map. A blue dot starts. Speedwell. O is cold and waits before following. Fear and Lothian. Does a live map have power to compel a body?

Is sand called sand in this port? Where did they bury the swan with the Spanish voice? ¡Olé! Anchors, ay, aye, and the signs tearing. Outside is bright and today means every day. Is the herring nice? Shall we try the hot sweet coffee? Light scuffs up behind swordsmen in an imaginary arena. The duel breaks down like pixels or biscuits, and stops being a thing. Crumbs. Laughter. Not the children's.

Here is the not-going-anywhere place. Buttons bleeping

inaudibly, thick ropes covered in mussels sometimes called muscles. Flesh. It goes and it comes, and the blink of an eye is a small shell that spins. O compass point. This is no-place. O sailors who never learnt to swim, looking at water, a dream of new clothes.

Far down the coast, a phantom German scoffs phosphorescent Suffolk herring; another, another country. Gobies wade through treacle; treacle wells through flint; out of a hole in the wall, macchiato coffee is a new drink in an old cup. The swan is a matchbox. Full of flares among angles. Light, light, come back. Up. From southern waters.

The children are on the move in their coats which are sails and their shoes which come off when they plunge down, down, into the laughing water. No waves, but walls all around. The children know where they must not go, so they change their names and keep going.

Call me a ringlet, call me a tongue tip dipped in salt; call me leaving forever, often called a wail. Do you hear it? The whales pay attention, opening the matchboxes to fold them into boats for lucky children to find. Over here! Over here! An old cup bobs on the surface; someone threw it over the line, saying coffee tastes better across the water. Would you say? A stain is a message in a blowhole. By the time it arrives, no need to drink; just admire. This was a song in several ports.

In those places which you have to get to, birds ignored by self-styled explorers hop on to the only remaining copy of the map. Singing guano, guano. Go. Now. You have to get past the going and arrive like a word with a conjectural ending, a bear, a bean, a bead.

Little house, little drips of hot water. That trying to find a place: quiet, still, far away from ropes, from the man who was lost and found the cabin door ajar, found the blue nightdress, found he was no match for infrasound, the low vibration turning sense data into false yet truly unbearable haunting. O, the portholes of his perception cracked with every emotion except his intent, lust. O, he forced himself to lie, to lie still, still he forced himself to lie, about his inability to take off other people's clothes. He could neither lodge nor dislodge, a lukewarm cockle, abominated. The blue nightdress lay, a small flag, its arms at rest like a saltire. O nobody's Alba, O all his nude lost land.

Sblood! The whaleroad spills mist into the little boat house, upstairs and downstairs, a see-saw, sighing. The children's interest in changing their names washes away. Guano! Guano! They are excited, too far away now to think of changing. Everything is turning in their worldport: the music on the radio, the thrum thrum that threw the man off the scent, the feverfew, the vetch. But O always remembers. Remembering is always backwards. A nose knows what is older, and sniffs out the fear of crying.

The children are young, their names little flagpoles waving to them in their nightdresses while they sleep. Lullaby lullaby, birds drop from the sky, nobody knows what country this is, not by the sound of a snore or the creak of a door, nobody knows whose, not cockle nor sailor nor nude. This country is nothing to do with them! Says who? Who made it? Who made it here? Them! Says the cry of the fishwife who has lost her armful of halibut, her lobster pot, the sweat from her brow. She's been missing for weeks! O, the sweet blue scent of children dreaming of shoes that walk over cobbles and know where the anchor is.

You can't want a port and not its ghosts. My shoulders are shaking now (says who?) and O is cold again (backwards backwards) ... Keep going, O! The ghost is or it isn't, and time is up. Or is it down with the moon and the shipwreck where the sound comes from? I don't know!

If you are caught in a current and pulled fast, if the current is time and you have your back to the past while being pulled backwards, your future looks longer but it's further away. Turn around, O! Haul anchor. Face the way you're going (backwards backwards). What, want a port and not its ghosts? How is making a living like being alive?

There's no walking forward as rapid as going back. The children always will be faster than you. You'll catch up with them by overtaking yourself. Now you are contemporary with the first port, which is anyone's home and nobody's country. Now the horizon is at your back, with the choir, the graveyard, the reclaimed future. Now you are now you aren't now you are now you aren't...

How often can you make the same entrance, or a different exit? Will you be late home? Late is early, if late is earlier than the ones who will be late. They got on the wrong ship with the wrong suitcases. That is not my dress! Chintz, chintz. They cry and wince at the moon going down. Coffee is nicer at home, but the exit is over there. The ropes are loose and you are all at sea with the clock going tock but not tick and (backwards backwards) .... Take the dresses off quick and find where to not be. Or at least where to not be seen (ghosts) and the sailors who could wake at any moment and catch you singing. Lulla lulla rock a bye, blood, blood, where did that come from?

Coffee is nice and new, shriek the beards. An egg is juicy and new, shriek the water rats. The fragile Japanese telescope to see the stars of Arabia and say sky in Irish is a funnel for all the alphabets that the folk who fetch up in this port own without the chance to learn. Singing comes before writing, and reading is reclaimed land. Put on a headdress from Amsterdam to find the centre where you can look back to heather ale, forward to rum. Are we in dresses? Are we going backwards, forwards, inside and out? Was the Ravenna Cosmography so, so wrong?

Read this ship. Give it a refresh. O, our dresses have eight sleeves and the largest hoods ever. The octomap is a sponge ball, and jelly wobbles on plates below deck. Can you hear it? Smell it slipping down your throat too easily? Get off the ship!

The children always happened before. They are after swimming in the dock. Their heads are on backwards, staring at the sun. A family consists of sized figureheads. The sailor's bird was an octowife, so what offspring can you expect? A port is not a colouring book. Land rats find port in love, death, and property ownership, without going to sea. Swans are elegant; cruel. Sugar and Ice are the swans that died in the night when the wall let the water in. The children melt in the brine and re-form. They run past the sign, tapping it with their beakpalms. They perch on the anchor stuck in the street.

Storm and sink and going going gone. Walk! Walk to Cramond and lie about Roman remains, let the houses live uninspected. About turn! Walk! Walk to the bright lights of Leith. Either way, the signs facing inwards say Haven. The country (which country?) is a blue speck edged in lace, a wave, a rivulet, O red and yellow rose bush. Only one is your true colour. (Says who?) Who dyed you? The rose that is called rose is no longer called rose but sleep, a little sleep, which is round; and the sand is called warmth, though there is no sand; and the beginning begins or is overtaken by the beaming lighthouse.

No sand, but a port is never over, and all the people are full of cold, but the sea is colder and fuller. So much swearing! Run instead, it's faster when you're hungry and want to push things out the door. You push the door but it's sealed in the ceiling. What are things? Why is a lighthouse like a writing desk? How does a buoy relate to a Tiffany lamp? Treasure is a hazard; light drops like setting concrete down the stairs, rain drops like sunlight, gold and blue.

Yo ho ho! A dead man sits up from his chest and returns a Newfoundland heart. It melts in the children's hands while the birds wait in their hard eggs. Wait, for arms to form on both sides, and downy hairs to tickle their new brown feet. Pink-eyed and unborn, they think too much about hatching to break out, and are gobbled by gulls.

Gulls and a blown fuse are the soundtrack, plus rats who live by lying and believe they know that singing is a trap. A haven, someone suggested? Whose children are these? Where do they live? A shriek is good for a change. Contort the mouth correctly and the sound comes out V-shaped, contort it wrongly and inhale a fog horn.

I didn't think we'd still be here, said the remaining boats to the reformulated waterline. Still. Again. Againstill said the waterline in its brand-new language. Then, hello, it says, do you like my woven collar? But nobody understands it. Not yet. Nobody is here to listen anyway.

Rats. Pirates. Romans. Nasturtiums. A pale-yellow tea. Lists I can manage, lists are a good way to learn a new language. Start with your pastimes: fishing, gutting, skinning, and immediately there's skin and blood and tiny little bones! But wait! This has nothing to do with the haven, the nesting birds, the quiet heat of radiators.

Skin is hard and easy. I watch it changing my face, making my eyes narrower. O, it is I, Master. Where are the children now they have all grown up. Have they grown up? The daughter of a poet staffs the café. The son of a fishmonger is a fishmonger. How colourful the boats are, how violent the noise of the gulls. Witch is witch? Sister Susie's setting storms for sailors. A haven for a raven, a sill for a gull.

I'm in the port, on tiptoe. It's like ballet, isn't it? I mean the shoes and having to keep moving, composed, moving, composed. A sheet of smiles stitched together billows over muscular pain. What a relief, says everybody at the same time, but they mean different things. Lie down and pull at curtains instead of mosquito nets. Can you remember, can you remember without looking if the sun is meant to be pale or yellow, mineral or animal, hot or bright? Don't look! Can you remember? No. The sun goes up or down behind the line of the sea, a line all salt fish and sunk crockery.

O, I went to sea, so far, too far, I couldn't stop! Pull me in, pull me in, cried my head, my feet, my cold wet legs. Children have chocolate; I was a child, too. But the cocoa tin lay rusting in the fisher's attic, and I flipped form and element, looking back with the warm brown eyes of a seal. Church bells rang. Deep resonance troubled my air the sea. I knew the way home. Sand and the concrete, the shouts of sons and daughters, the dim flickers of light in oblong windows. O, where is the anchor?

A huge tree sprawled like ball gowns. Ball gowns? Be careful what you wear, be careful what you climb up in your bare feet called feet, one after the other, one after the other. The tree might think you have married it, never to disentangle again, even if the reason you climbed it was to try out being human, you in your silver like the sea. O, I am speaking to you. A harbour is where voices call back.

Another comes after looking for single-meaning signposts (was there a willow? a bright yellow storm?), listening for whales, looking for an attic where a ghost made its nest, listening for… Go back, go back, go back! Time is a simple simultaneity reclaimed by memory from experience, like land from water. Words are a drowning. Nobody has to go to sea to find a port.

Tessa Berring and Vahni Capildeo

Foghorn (Stad)

The voice is low like me. Voice of a long time waiting. For a sea foreseen. Accidentally understanding threads of words is a form of confirmation. The river carves its way inland. A serrated perforation. New edges of bread–crumb. Blind alleys, valleys. The way the bridge "oats on, bobs its way to the bank and, there, hooded, lolls and loiters. Rubber lilypad on crested wave. The giant ship ploughs through, sounding its historical apology. What else could we do? Grabbing the hungry river   and   s h a k i n g it.
I commissioned a bridge high up and further away from the beginning of the water, more like what we're used to. A distant shortcut that bends into our various winds. Tethers and slats that take the weight of our backed-up traffic. Soundproof windows. We've always lived like this, trading a half for a quarter, smelling of calcium, sulphur, whatever we've been soiling. The ground cracks open and we make the most of it, bathing in the sudden saunas. Boiling eggs in mountain pools far from the wide open body. I want whales in here, frequenting the tunnels we've gone and provided. You said that if we scooped a lagoon, there would still be fauna. Still. We had to. There was always torpor. Voices of a long time waiting converge to make dough and only. The signage dying. The stem of the thistle (blown) I thought you were minding. Crouched in the extending estuary, two shells to two ears – a pearl in headphones – I hear the sea's coming back for another turn at the reins.

Lydia Unsworth

Little Egret / Tall Ship

A brief history of hunger

They are tearing up the trees from their place in muck and time along this here river – where once there were deep roots, now there is the low, echoing hum of machinery in the earth-belly; right where the land and the water make to merge.

There is a point along this river where I have experienced things I never imagined could happen here, here in this settlement of ancient oaks and healing strokes, in this border town, built on ancient bog-land, atop layer upon layer of loss.

The (two) things happened in different centuries from one another, on opposite banks of the same curve of the river's bruise-blue body; each at the polar ends which mark the fullness of one solitary day.

One event took its shape in the liminal space between this world and that other one which we cannot even seek to name, carved from false bone and marrow, sculpted as if it were a folkloric oak; by storm-fierce, imagined Atlantic winds.

The second thing was born wholly of that which is real, of blood and of feathers, of all things upright and breathing, collected and noted, stock-still – white as the snow, then, in a breath – all engaged in the fullness of flight, organic; so capable of dying.

*   *   *   *

[1] COFFIN SHIP

My hometown is the only place in the world, according to the learned writings of many, which, with authenticity, can tell the complete story of Irish emigration.

The scale, and indeed 'scéal'[1] of what that port town has

borne witness to remains – even to this day – without any proper or respectful record. We *know*, in that old Irish way, of course, without it having ever been written down. It has been passed down, over and over, a palimpsest of loss; '*Eisimirce.*'[2]

We know in our bones, in our marrow and in our flesh. We know in our skin and in our teeth. We know in our bellies, deeper than that; we know in our guts.

We know in our wombs. We know in our births and in our unborn.

We know in our living and in our breathing. We know in our leaving and in our dying. We know in our sleep, in our dreams and in our spaces in between these; we know in our thin places. We are '*The Children of the Famine*'.[3]

I awaken in a room, any room, any place; I awaken in places other than rooms. I awaken on the soil of my homeland, in my own town, on the side of the river I grew up on until the violence crept too close. I awaken in tents, on sand, in the arms of a lover, alone, on a train-plane-boat. I awaken on a wild island, in a vast and sprawling capital city, in a tree, during a monsoon. I awaken under sunset, I awaken at the turning point of the day; I awaken in the gap before the black night gives up its delicate ghosts.

I awaken. I awaken. I awaken.

---

1. 'Scéal' – The Irish word for Story.
2. 'Eisimirce' – The Irish word for Emigration
3. [Christine Kinealy]

I awaken from the same dream, over and over and over. I have long since dropped the threads that once kept count of the dream(s). Nae, it is not a series of 'recurring dreams' from which I awaken. It is the *only* dream, the same dream, *the* singular dream of my core. There is only *one* dream. It is the dream that drags me back up to the living world, kicking and screaming. I'll tell you the dream, shall I? *Beidh mé*.[4]

I am wearing tattered brown rags. I am dressed in the dirtied, peasant cloth(e)s of my ancestors. The night is darker than soot, blacker than a field of crows; ravenous birds trying to dig up the remnants of the crops that didn't come[5]; the phantom plant limbs of all that had failed us. The night is painted, tar like, with emptiness; loss seeps down from my very bones, through a garment that holds no hope of keeping out the cold. I am on a ship, not quite visible beneath the black sky, hidden under smog and freezing fog but still, despite it all; I know where I am. I know I am in a time long gone, a time I never witnessed with my own eyes. A time that, without having known, I have still, somehow known; *'Fado.'*[6]

I am the smallest and the last one to be let on the ship. I am weeping so hard that I can't walk in a straight line – my bony shoulders bash against the wet iron, the metal of the

---

4. 'Beidh mé' – Irish for 'I shall'. (There is no word in Irish for 'yes').
5. This speaks of the failed potato crop, often blamed for wiping out half of the Irish population during the famine. There are many unanswered questions about the idea that, in fact, this was an act of Genocide.
6. 'Fado' – Irish for 'Long ago'.

vessel seems sure to break me. And then, over and over, the dream shape-shifts and the quay, which was once, a mere moment ago, the departure point, has now become the destination. We are in Liverpool. We are in India. We are at the most North-westerly tip of Mull. We are in the whiteness at the bottom of Iceland. We are less than a mile further up the river whence we left. No matter where we are, the ship is always being thrown around in the blackness by waves sent from an unknown place. We are always told to jump – into the blackness, into the unknown, into the belly of the darkness.

In the dream that I have been having for decades now, I can feel the fear ripping my insides out and firing them up to the starless sky. I can trace my body's borderlines; I can see the death of me coming to meet the life of me in that thin place. But as I stand on that ship, looking out at the same point of the quay, the trauma comes to me in the same form. The trauma comes in the shape of hunger, always. A hunger that I cannot even name, a hunger that leaves me begging for the end, a hunger that makes me ready for the dying; *An Gorta Mór.*'[7]

I awaken from the dream, with the hunger still upon me; like a wolf.

The ship is a coffin ship. The port is my hometown. The loss is too brutal to comprehend. The ripples are felt throughout the land. We try to appease the dark waters

---

7. An Gorta Mór.' – The Irish for 'The Great Hunger', referred to outside of Ireland as 'The Potato Famine'.

with the bodies of our children, still; even now the river shares our hunger[8].

I awaken from the dream, with the hunger still upon me; like a wolf.

I am a child of the famine.

[2] WHITE BIRD

'Seacht'[9] is a very important, almost mythical number on this island: seven year cycles for Kings, seven bards, seven nobles, seven druids, seven coal black birds from seven little brothers, seven gates, seven rapes, seven sleeps, seven wakes; *'Seacht'*.

On the island of Ireland in the seven years between 1845 and 1852, the sound of the singing of the birds was replaced by a haunting, chilling, echoing silence. There is no room to discuss the dying of the birds. As for the humans, we try to put the shards of the story of their dying back together.

Those of them that could not find a way to leave their homeland on a tall ship went through a hunger the like of which I cannot even try to imagine. Those left behind that did not starve to death were worked to death, frozen to death or simply just lay down and gave in to the sorrow

---

8. Derry has one of the highest suicide rates in the UK. The River Foyle's role in this has been written of extensively. More of our lives have been lost in the North of Ireland through suicide now than were lost to the violence of the Troubles.
9. 'Seacht' – The Irish for the number 'seven'.

that seeped out through every single crack in the earth.

The earth in this port is cracking again. A new railway line is being built alongside the river, running parallel. The trees are gone now, as are the hedges. There is, again, no room to talk of the dying of the birds. The dredging up of the natural world has, like much that went before, also left deep scars[10].

The trauma of the land has thrown much up and out from the soil; the river's edges are strewn with debris the like of which its banks have never seen before. This newly sculpted edge-land of loss has carried curious gifts in its wake, somehow. I make my way across the bridge, my eyes drawn to the broken parts of the wild; piled up where the river meets the land. And there it is, that shock to my system, leaving me outside that very moment of time. There, in ethereal and beautiful whiteness, stands a Little Egret, hope being balanced in his bill. An otherworldly bird, brought right up to the building site at the mouth of the river, carried in the wake of all that was lost.

As I write this tale, the people of the port of Derry wait with bated breath to hear what their future holds, as a border town caught up in the trauma of Brexit, without their votes ever having been regarded whatsoever. There is, as of yet, no solution for the 'problem' of our border; that invisible line we have never even seen.

Yesterday, family members of peaceful protesters whose

---

10. "The famine was a defining event in the history of Ireland and Britain. It has left deep scars... Those who governed in London at the time failed their people." [Tony Blair].

lives were taken on a day painted the blood red of violence[11], were told only one person would be tried for the actions of so many more.

Just a handful of moments ago, I took my place in Guildhall Square with dozens of other peaceful protesters, using our voices to speak for the future, for our planet, for our home[12]. From where we stood we could see the River Foyle and the quay from which – not much more than a century and a half ago – we lost a million and a half of our kinfolk.

The young lad on the steps of the Guildhall is the only representative from his school at the protest. He stands, tall and defiant, upright against the biting winds, like that solo Little Egret in the silt.

This city is a city of history, he tells us. If the river we are standing right beside floods in 40 years time when the temperatures have risen too high, we will lose that history. We stand together, the child tells us, *"To preserve our history."*

We all cheer, many of us scream out at the top of our lungs, some of us weep. We are thinking of these children, the children of our future – of our present – the ones who are making history.

But as we cry out we are also paying our respects to those children that were lost, the children of our past. We are mourning them, as we stand there; we are laying to rest all of those children born 'outside history'[13].

---

11. The day spoken of here is 'Bloody Sunday' in 1972 when 14 peace protestors were murdered in Derry's Bogside by the British Army.
12. The Youth Climate Strike of March 2019.
13. [Eavan Boland].

[3] **BLACK POTATO**

'DÚCHAN' – blackening or darkening, black rust on potatoes, blight, sadness, oppression of spirits.
'DÚCHANN – song, refrain.
'DÚCHAS – birthright, ancestral home, also – wildness (of natural world).

*   *   *

The staff at the exhibition 'Coming Home: Art and The Great Hunger' in Derry, the final day of which was today, wrote to Glens of Antrim (the company that distribute the 'Irish Lumper' potato, the blight of which was 'to blame' for cutting the population of the island of Ireland in half in the middle of the 19th century).

The exhibition staff asked Glens of Antrim for 20 bags of potato seeds, in the hope that during the exhibition's span they would plant them in the rooftop garden of the building at workshops with local schoolchildren; the generation of children some scholars have termed 'The Last Children of The Famine'[14].

Instead of seeds, however, 20 boxes of harvested bags of potatoes arrived in their place. There are so many potatoes in the building today that they are being used as decoration for this weekend's upcoming St Patrick's Day festival.

---

14. Much research is available to read on the concept of the 'Genetic Imprint' of trauma on an inter-generational level.

The potatoes are piled upon one another as if they were small leaden bodies, the muck from the soil in which they were grown still clings to them like dirty rags; a reminder of all that lies beneath.

How could the company have ever understood such a request, what with the potato's history, in the light of so much inherited loss? Who could have ever, even nearly imagined that we could be ready, now; so overwhelmingly ready, *for the planting of seeds*[15] on our land once more?

Kerri ní Dochartaigh

---

15. The Irish word for healing, 'Íceach', finds its roots in the Irish word for planting.

The Wicked Capital

Tehran means reading never-ending Russian novels under my duvet,

glitterless gay parties until the morning Azan, until the birds scream,

mahogany cafés serving cinnamon tea and vanilla I scream,

Tehran is smoke and fury. It is fuming.

Tehran is static traffic, it is also fenugreek,

all-girl schools, all-boy love, and compulsory hijab,

and the evergreen Shahid Beheshti University where we exchanged

gay kisses but gay did not mean happy, it meant

homo whore harassed faggot corrupt beautiful.

The university whose rules we shattered in our attempts to

become Lord Byron. A university that is still shining, a neon

green sun in the north west of Tehran that inhaled our ashes, while we

smoked our youth and spat colonial classics, empowering ourselves.

(Now the question is: Will we ever be truly empowered? We,

the despondent snobs from the top universities of Iran, who ended up in the bottom

universities of Brexitland, Dumpland, The North Pole, doing degree after

degree after degree so we/they can forget our skin colour and forgive

our accent even though we are pale like flour, and quiet

like infected parrots, will we ever be empowered?)

In Tehran we are still powerless, even though

it is officially our homeland: our sealess port.

Tehran, the harbour of pollution where fast cars screech

American pop in ambivalent alleyways paved with martyrs' blood.

I have never seen a city capable of containing so much love and hate.

Tehran is my parents and our house,

my siblings and my best friend, his passion

for beautiful boys and avant-garde theatre, and the scenario

of our eternal escape. Tehran is my grandmother,
cherry pickles that she made just for me with specifically
rotten sour cherries that surprisingly tasted like god,
her God that was not my god and became a gap that devoured our love.
Tehran is my real room, my bookshelf, my vanity table, crowded
with bottles of blue varnish – my first rainbow flag.
Tehran is aromatic; herbs, saffron, dried lime,
turmeric, salt, bloody beans, red meat, brown flesh.
After Persian cuisine, nothing tastes great.
Tehran is Arabic prayers and Persian poetry:
Bookshops floating in the sizzling summer streets:
Forough Farrokhzad, Sohrab Sepehri, and Sadegh Hedayat, but also
preposterous books such as bad translations of
American self-help and Mein Kampf,
everything for a cheap price. And the everlasting question:
How can this country survive when Hedayat
killed himself and Forough died at such a young age?

Tehran is fear. More wars, more sanctions, more inflation.
The morality police. Our government, the US government, Saudi Arabia,
and the government of Israel. Fear of all the governments, and fear of more chaos
Fear of expenses. Fear of being stuck. Fear of leaving. And of returning.
Fear of missing. Fear of losing and fear of winning.
Fear of anarchy, and love of anarchy.
And love.

Living in Tehran is like being in love with the villain
everyone judges and wonders why, but one will not
lower oneself to explain the attraction.
The moment anything is justified, it becomes boring, common, worldly.
This is why when people ask where in Iran I am from,

I respond, *the wicked capital*,

saturated with gold oil, dripping with black glory,

come in but stay out, so you won't regret it.

Golnoosh Nour

Or Bridport Harbour, if you like. The world's heritage in silt and shingle. A small harbour repaired and moved twice. First sited further inland, then relocated to the East Cliff, then a few hundred metres west to where it lies today. A small port town of rope and nets, and yards to build frigates, cutters, schooners, brigantines, barques and fishing smack. But change was transported in with industry's surge. Steam-powered vessels had no need for the ropes of sailing ships, and then the railway arrived, and the port was rebranded as a resort, with villas and lodging houses built in the styles of northern France and the Arts and Crafts Movement. The cliffs made of Frome Clay and Forest Marble became fashionable for their horizontal banding and their fossils. And today the webcam live streams from the harbour master's office, lingers on the bobbing fishing and pleasure craft. And along the promenades tourists huddle in cagoules, struggle with umbrellas. The sea breaks white and the flags blow. An ambulance idles in the car park. It is August, after all.

The Liverpool Spectre

Her empty eyes blinded by the smack
of sweetness gunning messages through sea
fret. Ships calculated with ballast
weigh down her feet. Her breaths
conjure centuries; she hears tears from waves
of knives that split the sugar cane.
A singular woman, middle passage slave,
births in manacles, she pays and pays.
On shore her master's iron bust
while her ears turn to rust.
Sunbird songs and magical notes,
echoing drums – ancestral voices.
Salt-bleached as brig-rigged planks,
her scorched skin drifts
                like dry sand.

Moira Garland

Whitehaven

I never found fairy rock. Even its name was lost to me for years, washed away with voices also gone. But on the edge of a solid-set Georgian port in the far northwest of England, in a county that rarely gets a national mention, and in a fringe of the county that often gets overlooked, or plain bypassed, or never reached, fairy rock is there to this day, and despite some of it being lost to a storm in 1872, if you know where to look, its remains can still be found, balanced precipitously on a coastal cliff that refuses to wholly give way to the currents of the Irish Sea.

As the legend goes, Fairy Rock, near the old colliery of Saltom Pit, is the site where the last fairy was spotted in Whitehaven, Cumbria. Once, fairies lived in grottoes here. They were human-sized, wore white robes, and when they danced in the moonlight their feet left no trace on the earth. The fairies were peaceful but mischievous, living in harmony with their local human neighbours and inviting handsome young men to their dances.

In the 17th century, one such man from St Bees, a handful of miles round the sandstone headland from Whitehaven, fell in love with and married the queen of the fairies. But, as fairies are tricksome folk, he was only allowed to visit her at Fairy Rock on days when the moon was full. Over time, the man's jealousy and desire steadily increased, and he set out by boat to see the Fairy Queen on an unallotted day. As he journeyed round the headland, a storm broke, his boat was capsized and he drowned. It is said that sometimes, if you listen carefully, you can still hear the fairies singing by the rock.

Saltom Pit was the first undersea coal mine in Cumbria. It operated between 1730 and 1848, officially being opened in 1732 to a great celebration. Protected for many years, it is now being left to the wind and the rain and the sea, to gradually slip from sight, into the salt and into the past.

Squint a little, though, and its remains tell of a lost world. A sandstone winding house; a chimney for the fires; a gin circle

to pump out the mine shaft and raise the coal; the head of the
shaft itself now covered with concrete and cased in metal; the
footings of engine houses and miners' dwellings; boiler sheds;
shops; a coal depot.

Saltom's mine shaft was elliptical – half was used for pumping
out water, the other for drawing up coal from beneath the sea
bed. The arm of the gin that turned the winding drum was
powered by horses, until the introduction of the Newcomen
Engine, which could power the machinery by steam. A
tramway carried coal from the mine to nearby Ravenhill Pit,
where it was transferred to Whitehaven harbour.

Whitehaven had been a harbour of at least some commercial
import since the early 16th century – there are records of quay
dues – wharfage – dating from 1517. But it was when the
Lowther family purchased the manor of St Bees in 1630,
that Whitehaven started to build its reputation, along with
whatever wealth it made, through the export of coal. Sir
Christopher Lowther's stone pier, built between 1631 and 34,
survives in modified form as the Old Quay today.

Over 300 years, more than 70 coal pits were sunk in
Whitehaven and the surrounding area. Now there are no
working mines. The machinery and tramlines and ships full
of coal, that made Whitehaven harbour a blackened sooty
place as late as the 1980s, are all gone. In 1983, a geological
fault was found at Haig Pit that endangered, and increased
the cost of, operations there. And then there was the miners'
strike in 1984–85. Whitehaven's miners fought to open a new
coalface, but it was too late, and by 1986 Whitehaven's coal

mining history had reached its end.

In 1992, the harbour lost its last commercial cargo handling operation, when the Marchon chemical plant, situated on the headland between Whitehaven and St Bees, stopped importing phosphate rock. The working port was redeveloped, the harbour's inner basins impounded, creating a leisure and fishing marina that shows little signs of its industrial past.

The fortunes of ports can change in slow motion or at double speed, or at both simultaneously. Whitehaven's pier suffered storm damage in the 1660s. The impervious becomes not so impervious. By the 1670s the growing number of vessels wanting to dock in the harbour outstripped capacity and the harbour was extended with extra ballast walls, breakwater moles and piers. Architecturally it became one of the most interesting and complex harbours in Britain.

Trouble arrived, too. In April 1778, during the American War of Independence, American ships under the command of John Paul Jones, sometimes known as the Father of the American Navy, planned an assault on the harbour, hoping to torch and sink all Whitehaven's vessels. The attack was thwarted, however, after the American landing party opted to visit a local hostelry for a drink, delaying them until dawn, by which time the the townsfolk had been alerted. They thronged to the harbour and forced the Americans to retreat.

In the 19th century, the west coast ports of Bristol and Liverpool, with their larger capacities, took trade from Whitehaven. The port's survival became dependent on local mining for coal, and for haematite that was used to make steel. Innovation in the steel industry reduced the need for West Cumbrian haematite, however, and in the 20th century, Irish independence saw the creation of tariff barriers on Whitehaven coal's major export market.

Back to the coal face and the harbour blackened with soot. More than 1,700 men, women and children, lost their lives in Whitehaven's collieries – this from a population that has averaged around 20,000. On 11 May 1910, 136 men and boys died during the Wellington Pit disaster. After a large initial explosion, fires continued to burn in the mine. Everyone trapped in the shafts below the sea was presumed dead, and the only way to extinguish the fires was to seal off the mine with the miners still underground.

Wellington Pit stayed sealed all summer, until in September the gruesome job of recovering bodies began. Distressingly, chalked messages were found, showing that many miners had survived the explosion. Only 12 had been killed outright by the blast. Official records tell that the rest perished from burns, shock and suffocation. Three bodies were never identified. Not all the bodies were recovered.

Between 1922 and 1931 four separate explosions killed 83 workers at Haig Pit. Again, decisions were taken to seal off the mine shafts. In 1947, 104 men were killed in the William Pit disaster. Miners are still entombed here, out beyond the harbour walls, deep under the sea. And for every lost miner another widow, more grieving parents, fatherless children, poor families without an income, a town in shock and silence, a sense of tragedy that lingers even now when the events of these years are recalled. The losses a place endures, the times that a town gives up its own.

In 2019, a bright orange vessel is moored in Whitehaven's rejuvenated marina. *Tenacity* is a rapid crew transfer vessel designed for a growing offshore wind industry that is gradually being located further out into the Irish Sea. From fossil fuels to renewables in a matter of decades.

Is it a clear sight of a cleaner, safer future along West Cumbria's 'Energy Coast'? Plans have also been approved for a new undersea coal mine, out from Whitehaven along the coast to St Bees. It seems old habits die hard. Councillors, predictably, have applauded the project for the jobs it will create. Environmentalists, predictably, are mounting their opposition.

Do those who arrive in their pleasure craft think of a port's history? Do they think of the ships that once came to Whitehaven's Queen's Dock? The Sea Cadets who gathered along the Old Quay? The derivation of the names of Lime Tongue and Sugar Tongue? The long protecting arm of the West Pier? What of the crumbling cliffs of South Beach, with the old colliery's candlestick chimney still pointing skyward above?

I grew up in West Cumbria, just a few miles down the coast, but I've not lived there since 1989, which means it sometimes feels like it's only part of my past, too. But I still sometimes re-tread formative steps along the pier and to South Beach, looking for the place I've never quite located as being Fairy Rock, but where banks of cloud and rain can roll in seemingly out of nowhere, in no time at all. South Beach where the sea and sky seem to merge so easily, so often. South Beach that looks out to the headland of St Bees, where the sea makes its legends, where folklore lies at rest, with the sea that claims what it thinks is its own – stories that slip from sight, out into the salt and the past.

Of course Whitehaven is not the past, it is those who are there now – those who will take this solid-set Georgian port forward in the 21st century; those who may never know the smell of coal; those who rebel against nostalgia; those whose departures continue so they can make a life elsewhere, and those who have arrived in the town to make it their home.

When people say they are proud of their town, what do they mean? Are people proud of Whitehaven? To be honest, I'm never quite sure. I think I would be. But maybe the question is wrong. What is certain, however, is that the past has made Whitehaven a remarkable town. It's also a place that feels wary of the lure of false promises, wary of being let down, and steeled for the storms that might come.

MW Bewick

Mackerel & Slipways

Though some said otherwise,
I was struck by the elegance of mackerel
swimming amongst reflected birds,
when a wave turned us into the Clyde.

Slipways of The Old Yard were caught
between gasps for air and the airless depths;
rigging and tumbling oars, tossed in bubbles
with graceless fear… and blackness.

I am floating now, liberated by parting skies,
beyond hogback stones and the old kirk walls
where heavy bells toll for the cost of living;
nineteen lives lost for a halfpenny ticket.

Fleshless mackerel bones etched in riverbanks,
slipways slipping towards inevitability –
relics of former glories, where ships
that came to pass, no longer pass this way.

Waning moon in Scorpio, 2018

*In memory of the 19 men who drowned in the
Govan ferry disaster, 30th November 1864.*

Gary Liggett

The General Synopsis at Midday

It has been hallucinations since the Douglas Complex of gas and oil rigs, although the bright blue shooting stars and the puffin outriders port side were real enough. The moon casts shadows, which is unexpected, but not as unforeseen as chimneys blowing smoke in the middle of the sea; these of course exist only in our own imaginations. As the sun comes on watch, the fuzzy mass of the Isle of Man rises from the waves. It seems to be alight, coruscating copper orange licking the edges of the cliffs, a purplish patina appearing above.

I'm at the mast, uncleating the halyard then easing the mainsail down towards me, flaking it first, then strapping it to the boom with white ribbons and Flemish knots, grasping hard myself as the bow muddles through a patch of rough. As we prepare to make landfall, the realisation strikes that we are off course by a number of degrees. The sea will never let you create a desire line – its tides dictate which path you follow despite your best efforts at civil disobedience. We recalibrate our approach and blurs take shape and become solid entities and suddenly there is Man's capital – its futuristic ferry terminal, its Tower of Refuge ramparts, its red blinking concrete dolphin. Marking the end of the Battery Pier breakwater, this warns unsuspecting mariners of naturally occurring overfalls where currents collide. The devil is in the detail.

It is almost midday on Wednesday, almost 24 hours since we locked out in the shadow of those liver birds, under the watchful eyes of the cardinal buoy cormorants; almost 24 hours since we spoke to anyone other than our crew of two, us. Now, the male voice on Channel 12 tells me we have to wait for the flap-gate to be lowered and the road bridge to be manoeuvred before we can access the pontoons of the marina; our new home, at least for a short while. The window of opportunity is two hours either side of high water, depending on land-based traffic – he is hopeful about getting us through before the lunchtime rush hour. Until then, it's a case of swanning about in the outer harbour, avoiding the Steam Packet, or tying up on Battery's temporary berth.

I fetch fenders and work on persuading my fingers to manipulate their ropes into repeated round turns and two half hitches. It's easier said than done, but the call comes through and we're on, inching our vessel into place, me jumping ship onto the diving board jetty and grappling the sheets onto cleats without stumbling or swearing, making out I've done this before, many times. There's an audience gathered above our heads, absentmindedly picking at paper packets of chips, eyes glued, before dissipating back up the narrow streets away from the slip, back into the bosom of the town. You cut the engine and silence descends, just the slapping of water at the Plimsoll line, the shouting of seagulls bouncing off the high harbour walls.

54° 08.9N, 04° 28.0W

Noon, Tuesday. We're up on Marine Drive, which teamed with tourists in those halcyon days of late Victoriania thanks to its groundbreaking electric tramway and engineering feats of ironwork bridge spans at Horse's Leap and Pigeon Stream power house and re-purposed funicular lifts. A crenelated triple-arched toll gate built by the men behind Blackpool Tower guards the entrance to the scenic route, doffing a cap to Llandudno. Both the Pleasure Beach and the Great Orme are 63 miles from here if traditional transportation methods were embarked upon to flee.

Sea side there are sheer drops of layered slate and scree-slathered steep slopes; land side, it's buckled strata exposed to the elements, topped with coastal fields. The wind can be fierce here, and the Manx choughs and wagtails don't hang about. Clinging on for dear life in the hellish cliff-edge gusts is sulphur-coloured gorse and flaming orange Lucifer. Honey-scented heather and burnt-toast bracken squat on the higher tussock mounds and hillsides. These are the fires I caught sight of from my crow's nest. My back is turned to the view expanding outwards from the Camera Obscura across the harbour and lighthouse north towards the Solway Firth. I'm heading south, wondering about the future for the former pleasurelands of Port Soderick, once upon a time all segregated swimming areas, bathing huts, dance halls and fancy eateries. The sky-blue painted paddling pool has filled with pebbles; the fairy glen's guesthouse buildings are dilapidated and derelict, fit only for demolition. Where once there were sea lions in enclosures, now only a sea fret rolls in, trapping me from casting off and heading on to the Holy Island adrift in Welsh waters.

It is July going into August but even so the colour-saturated postcards in salt-rusted metal display racks down on the front don't ring true. Deposited back in Douglas, like the shingle pushed by the tide into Port Soderick's concrete crevices, I leave the Ruabon red station, start and end point of the longest narrow-gauge steam railway in Britain. Across the street lolls the Tongue Building, with its chart-packed chandlery and sump-smelling marina offices; its all-important blue-glossed noticeboard displaying the latest shipping forecast and lifting bridge timetable. Calm conditions are promised; an escape is on the horizon. The moment to ready for departure is upon us; we check the radio. The capital's population of 27,938 mill about their business as we wander down to the prom going about ours, dodging clattering horse-drawn trams, another of the island's unique infrastructure solutions. We're off in search of a final fish supper in one of the pubs, still smoky in spite of the recent mainland ban. Our other task is to commit to memory the names of the hotels whose grand bay windows give out onto the Irish Sea: the Empress, the Sefton, the Ascot, the Claremont, the Regency. They'll be useful later for willing on sleep, before the rude awakening to catch the tidal gate lowering when even the sun hasn't given a thought to rising.

Sarah-Clare Conlon

A westerly point of rocky shoreline, where cultures collide in the surrounding marshlands and summits, on the mainland and beyond. Here pilgrims come in the footsteps of 20,000 saints. In the ruins of an old abbey stands a Celtic cross. Wonder at a Roman anchor, a Neolithic axe, a Mesolithic flint. Bardsey Island like a comet, like a whale, always present, always like it's passing. Under a cairn on a hilltop lies the giant, Odo Gawr. Nearby, the rock known as Carreg Samson, thrown from Uwchmynydd by Samson himself – the holes in the rock the imprint of his fingers. Underneath the rock, a pot of gold. What drew Samson out here to the edge of the Atlantic? What drew the saints? What created the need for these stories? Life and nature entwined at the edge of a known world. In the 15th century, the poet Dafydd Nanmor, in 'Gwallt Llio', writing of the rocks at Uwchmynydd, coloured by their covering of golden lichen, the colour of a loved one's hair. Beyond, only the ocean.

The Sank Ports

They named North and South Shields after the sheds on the banks of the river. The fishermen lived in the sheds: some on the north bank of the Tyne and some on the south bank. This was a world of wild cabbage. Things were bloody bitter.

These dry days you rarely find anyone talking about East, West and Middle Shields, though they were the big three for about 250 years.

Middle Shields was a rocky outcrop in the middle of the Tyne's gaping mouth. There was only ever one family living there. The Fernandez clan was tolerated, even celebrated by some, but there was something about each and every one of them that sparked fear. The yellow and green jerseys with the embroidered number nine. The neat beards. The absence of shin pads even when they went to *The Jungle* as that pub was known.

West Shields was more of a political movement than a place: an attempt by those living near the mouth of the river to show their importance and try to lord it over Newcastle by changing the name of the neighbouring city. It was partially successful for about three hours.

East Shields was an island so far out to sea it had regular arguments with lots of ocean-going ships. It eventually lost its moorings, its bearings and its way. At the back end of the 18th century, a steam cruiser heading for Norway had double-booked a number of its rooms, so picked up East Shields on the way over. The extra passengers slept in the crew's rooms and the crew slept on the island that was expertly towed behind the *Alexander and Margaret.*

There was an amnesty in the 1970s whereby all the canny folk of all the canny Shields, past and present, were invited to bury hatchets they never possessed in gardens they'd never dreamt of. They built a memorial to all these lives between the piers and oafishly placed it on the river bed.

Rob Walton

The Merchant of Dreams

I trade in dreams

     I pour them like a perfect arc
of golden tea the mayor's wife serves to her guests.
She smiles as they comment on the sweetness
of her gingerbread, is triumphant when they gasp
at her centrepiece: a pineapple – that strange,
scaled fruit, rarer than a dragon's egg.

     I whisper them like a rustle
of silk into the new bride's ear as she sits up
in rumpled India cotton sheets. She sips
chocolate, négligée sliding from
the bitten peach of her shoulder.

     They swirl like smoke around
the student's head as he lolls on a bunk
in a Limehouse den. Swifter than wind
in a clipper's sails, he's carried to the *Celestial Empire,*
pupils dilated like a poppy's black heart.

     They itch like the cuntstruck sailor
as he staggers down the gangplank, heading
for the woman who waits in a red-lit room.
He'll fill her with camellias and parakeets,
kimonos and the clap, the tattoo of his
other 'wife' flexing as he thrusts.

I set them loose like rats that spill
from the hold and into the night, oozing
like tar. Brazen, one skitters, chittering
over the dandy's buckled shoe as he sidesteps a turd,
making for the women that line the alley's walls.

My dreams hover like the mother
who waits in the night's slow hours, watching over
her babe. She sponges rings of red spots,
prays her child will live to sing and dance in circles,
laugh at the word 'atishoo'.

Alex Toms

Pint, Port

Somewhere in the world it's early in the morning. And somewhere in the world, in an early morning airport terminal, while locals blearily wheel their luggage towards the coffee concession, there will inevitably be at least one man gleefully drinking a pint of lager.

This is a universal law of nature. Next time you're passing

through an airport, look out and you'll see it. And it isn't just confined to the provincial home bases of quick-and-dirty stag party-friendly airlines; it happens absolutely everywhere there's an airport bar or café, from Marrakech to Malaga, Shanghai to San José, Portland to Prague.

Our asynchronous drinker (often alone, occasionally part of a small party) may well be smartly dressed, in a businesslike shirt, and propped by their chair leg will be a laptop bag with a vaguely familiar corporate logo stitched on to it, picked up at a conference or seminar. Maybe that's what they're coming back from, or maybe they're going to another one.

They aren't raging alcoholics or stressed-out self-medicators. These are the sort of people who wouldn't dream of picking up a beer at breakfast time when at home. But the fact that here they are, enjoying a refreshing Carlsberg or Efes or Sam Adams, says something quite interesting about the world now and how we travel around it.

The classic idea of the port – you were probably wondering when the subject would finally come up – is of a fascinating, dangerous, confusing place where cultures mixed, deals were done, both dishonestly and not, and continual embarkations to barely heard-of foreign destinations gave it an exotic quality – both part of its country and semi-detached, as though some of those other, connected places had started to leak into its fabric.

William Gibson's clever near-future novel *Neuromancer*

started with this excellent line: "The sky above the port was the color of television, tuned to a dead channel." The book itself, interestingly, has not survived into its own future terribly well; some of its predictions were astonishingly prescient, many well wide of the mark. But that use of the word 'port' in the first line immediately sets the tone. We're in a place of possibilities and potential. A port.

That is usually taken to mean a seaport town; the first type of travel terminus, one that endured for centuries and gave a unique character to so many cities. San Francisco, Liverpool, Marseille, Hong Kong and more were defined by their harbours and docks.

But where are the seaports now? Cargo has been shovelled into Lego-brick containers, robotically unloaded many miles upstream in a featureless concrete facility. And people don't travel by sea any more, unless they're being herded on to a short-haul ferry or coach-driven to an out-of-town cruise ship terminal.

Nowadays most of the docks themselves are upmarket shopping and socialising venues, or office spaces, or recreational waterparks. The ships have gone. The seaport city as a functional place of work and commerce is no longer part of our world. That type of port is just a historical memory of funnels and masts in blurry black and white.

People still travel by train, though. And the railway station was almost, for a while, the seaport's equivalent in glamour and possibility. Even now, standing in one of the great European cathedrals of steam, gazing at destination boards featuring the grandest cities of the continent still brings a frisson of dizzying potential. Should you board the express to Budapest or Berlin and start a new life? Change your appearance, change your name, begin again in Prague, Pisa or Paris?

Talking of Paris, you probably hate Johnny Hallyday, the weirdly-cheekboned 'French Elvis'. And you'd be right, mostly. Some of his musical output makes Cliff Richard look as hip as Nick Cave. But there's one thing he did which just sort of worked. In 2002 he was, oddly, cast in a film called *L'Homme du Train*, or *The Man on the Train*. He plays a past-it bankrobber, a role for which his rather odd, unearthly looks somehow fitted him well. He gets off a train in a small French provincial town, randomly meets a local academic, and… well, you'll have to watch it.

Its first major plot point, though, is all about that sense of possibility that a train journey has; the idea that a whole other life is possible by getting off at a different station or taking a new branch line. Maybe *Sliding Doors* is the ultimate expression of that – a world of alternative universes just a train ride away.

But a railway station just doesn't have the sprawling exoticity of a seaport. It can't. It's too confined, too rooted in place by its iron rails. Some stations, to be fair, did spawn their own transient-friendly districts of rough hotels, cheap cafés and grubby bars where nobody was actually drinking by choice. The area around London's King's Cross, St Pancras and Euston used to be your best bet for getting into a fight with an incomprehensibly furious Scot or a Mancunian with a chip on his shoulder and a zipped-up cagoule. And hanging around the Gare du Nord in Paris used to be a good way to learn the latest Moroccan drug slang and some fascinatingly ingenious ways to separate unwary travellers from their belongings. But King's Cross is now just a sea of blandly upmarket retail opportunities and even the Gare du Nord is no longer actively dangerous unless you get in the way of a determined Chinese tour guide.

And railways are much too workaday and sensible. For every Trans-Siberian Express or Blue Train there's a myriad of humdrum commuter 18:07s to Bromley South or Nuneaton. Today's stations are mostly an unlovely mess of chain retail opportunities, slabbily functional architectural add-ons and corporate clutter. The magic which hung around them in the days of Eric Ambler, Graham Greene and John Buchan has dispersed, along with the clouds of steam and pipe smoke. The only spies you're likely to run across at Birmingham New Street are mystery shoppers in Prêt à Manger.

So where does that leave us? In the bar, of course. Which is never a bad place to be left, even if it is very early in the morning, you're in an airport, and on the next table somebody is drinking a pint of lager.

The airport is, of course, not exactly a nexus of cool itself nowadays. Its days of behatted gents and carefully coiffured ladies arriving at Croydon, Orly or Tempelhof and being shown to a comfortable wicker armchair to sip Krug and watch the co-pilot swinging the prop of a biplane are long gone. The model for modern airport design is the identikit international mall – blandly useful shops, chain catering and familiar brands' outlets. The idea seems to be that wherever in the world you are, it'll feel comfortingly familiar. And comfortingly profitable for the airport operators – nearly half of their income comes from 'non-aeronautical' sources, which is to say renting out retail units and/or taking a cut of operators' profits.

But they're not all like that yet. Some airports still have their own identities. Watching the rugby in the bar at Derry airport, armed with a pint of Murphy's, while estuary squalls batter the windows is a splendid thing. Boggling at the display of knives in Geneva, while being informed amiably that it's perfectly OK to take them on your flight, is scarily unusual. The shoulder-padded 1980s Thatcherite vibe of London City is oddly fascinating.

Even some bigger airports still defy the norm, like the roiling shambles of Rome Fiumicino, which clings on to its frustrating, dysfunctional, distinctively Italian character. It's possible to count 25 different kinds of immaculately tailored uniform there, all accessorised with plenty of gold braid and excellent sunglasses, but nobody has the faintest idea what's going on.

In an airport, unlike a seaport or a station, it still feels as though there are possibilities. That departure board offers up a far larger number of intriguing destinations than even the greatest shipping almanac, and easily beats a railway's earthbound local selection. If you have the money, you can still turn up and buy a last-minute ticket to somewhere far away and thoroughly foreign due to a sudden whim or a vital mission.

Geography has been beaten; the globe is now nothing more than a pick-and-mix menu to be experienced, consumed and ticked off a list. But there's one extra, remarkable thing about the airport which thoroughly merits its place at the apex of today's travel (until they build spaceports, of course. Which, sadly, are more likely to be dehumanised high-tech transit facilities for squirting stunned astronauts into orbit than the charmingly ramshackle 1930s-Shanghai-with-rockets-and-wizards of *Star Wars*).

Not only has distance been rendered largely irrelevant by commercial flight but – and this is important – so has time. Thanks to the fact that we cling to a spinning pebble revolving around a distant star, the people you see getting off planes or changing flights may quite literally not be in the same moment as you. For them it's late morning, or early evening, or the middle of the night in the case of the most dishevelled and disorientated. Not only is it possible to be confused about where you are, but when you are. The question becomes not just 'what time is it?' but 'what time is it where?'

If you're travelling frequently for short periods, or you're en route to somewhere else, one well-worn tactic is to ignore the actual time at your temporary stop-off point and hold tight to your familiar temporal landmarks. Whatever the state of the sun or moon it makes sense to head for somewhere away from natural light and hang on to your own routine.

Somewhere like an airport bar, for instance. Where, whatever the time may say on nearby clocks, it quite possibly feels like early evening. There's a few hours to kill before the next flight, so what do you do? Sit and quietly marvel at the ability of mankind to totally eradicate the barriers of distance and time, while inhabiting the ultimate expression of a space that is both somewhere and nowhere in four dimensions?

No. Order a pint of lager. Seems only sensible.

Chris Maillard

Alexandria

They placed a glass at the apex of stone.
One hundred metres high, a glinting
speck that called the horizon home.

At night they'd make a siren of their fire
to flare that men at sea might find its light.
A guide like love that shone and far.

Foreign books that came in, they'd confiscate
for the written word to them was a map
to weigh men's souls. The freight

one phrase might bring, a kind of contraband.
Such stuff could not be given back, but kept
safe for time or gold, a theft of minds, unplanned

and yet, in their possession of the page
a design to shape what no man had glimpsed,
nothing less than the earth's disc pixelate in space.

Imagine this: like a god looking down
at the dodecahedron of the world
to fix the colours to that unmapped ground.

Michael Brown

South of The Point, the language of legends persists where the roughest winter storms and swells have sought to wreck the smooth lineage of time. A Tudor quay stood here until the late 19th century, when finally the pier head and wall were destroyed, leaving only formation stones that can be glimpsed at low tide. And so the Customs House becomes a hotel. Corn and haylofts are its bedrooms. Stables become a bar. Fishermen's cottages are a toilet block. A museum, brimful of memorabilia of lives and times lost. The steamship *Uppingham*, stranded under Longpeak. SS *Rosalia* angled sharply across the rocks. Or the 80ft wooden sailing vessel *Zuma*, built and registered in Sunderland in 1851, re-registered in London, and then in Guernsey, wrecked at Hartland Quay, on a voyage from Bilbao to Swansea, with a cargo of iron ore. And then all the names of the captains, masters and crew that have also slipped away. What remains is the cliff face like geometry, the tempest-furrowed shore, the visitors arriving, looking on.

Lord Ashton's Common

Walking towards the quayside of the River Lune, Lancaster has the distinct feeling of a northern city half-forgotten in the regeneration projects. Lines of the well-known ex-miners cottages, grey and with graffiti scrawled onto the brickwork of nearby railway bridges, lead onto the riverside road.

Closer to the town centre the old industrial buildings have been renovated into brightly lit flats, not too far off the standard you might find by the Thames, but cross under the bridge and the abandoned remains of the rest of Lancaster's industrial and maritime past still lie empty. The echoing buildings had been left to decay for decades, but now, from the other end of the river, gradually they are torn down to make way for a sprawling estate of new-builds.

Lancaster worked hard to establish itself as a port. The Lune River was straightened and cleared. It took it's part in the bloody history of the British Empire, beginning to carve out it's place in the late 1700s. For a short time Lancaster was the fourth largest slave trading port in England. Much of the city centre was developed rapidly, built on the men, women and children traded across the Atlantic like cattle.

These heady days quickly crumbled when the slave trade was abolished in 1807. After a few flourishing decades the river began to silt up and Lancaster slipped into a more modest position as the northern powerhouses of the industrial revolution took hold.

However, the docks around the now diminished port still thrived. The Williamson family were one of the most prominent to take over what remained of the quayside. James Williamson, eventually becoming Lord Ashton, expanded the family's fabrics company into the production of linoleum. As he bought up property, including bankrupt shipyards and the site of old brickworks, Williamson created a virtual monopoly on this lucrative new material, growing to become the largest factory of its kind in Europe.

The port served him well, with cork shipped directly from Spain and Portugal, as did the town's workforce. Around a quarter of the men were employed in his factories along with a large number of the women. It seems most, apart from his more skilled labourers, were underpaid and unionisation was strongly discouraged.

Like many entrepreneurs, Williamson used his fortune, grown from the exploitation of workers, on setting up a public image of the philanthropist while also making his mark on the city. His money put a bronze statue of Queen Victoria in Dalton Square and he had constructed the impressive Ashton Memorial, overlooking the city in the grounds of Williamson Park, among many other donations.

One of his more disputed gifts is the land that has become Freeman's Wood. The plot stands at the end of the road that hugs the riverside and was previously used as the tip for the linoleum factory. Having ravaged the area, it is claimed that Williamson donated this site to the people of Lancaster in 1907.

In the century or so that followed the waste was gradually reclaimed as the trees dug their roots through layers of accumulated rubble. Greenery of all kinds flourished, and the woods became an idyllic retreat for residents from every corner of the city. It became a piece of common land, shared by generations. Football pitches and cricket grounds were erected on the greens. Walkers, foragers, birdwatchers and adventurous children took advantage of the haven of the woods.

But in 2011 the commons were unexpectedly usurped.

Coming into the woods from the main road the change was at first veiled by the trees. Walking through footpaths winding towards the centre of the woods, alongside farmland and a gentle stream, the grey steel of fences gradually rise through the greenery.

What once was common is now cut off, footpaths blocked by signs of 'No Trespassing, Private Property'. Behind them the earth and trees have been ripped up and the long buried remnants of Williamson's legacy are unearthed. Garish blue of linoleum waste is mixed with the brown and green of the land. The mounds pile up as high as the fences protecting them.

The woods have been passed between various companies' hands, a splurge of corporate pass-the-parcel which began in 1971 when the council first sold it off. But the people won't give up their land as easily as the council.

There have been brief occupations, long-running legal disputes and council applications resisting the enclosure. Many of the signs were quickly defaced. With seemingly no attempt to remove the rebellious graffiti, it becomes clear how distantly interested the Bermuda-based owners are in this land that they have earmarked for property development. The new signage ranges from the direct, 'No More Land Grabs You Thieves', to the more poetic quoting of old union songs:

They hang the man and flog the woman

That steals the goose from off the common

But let the greater villain loose

That steals the common from the goose.

The potential fate of Freeman's Wood oddly echoes the life of its fabled donor. As the unions and the Labour Party grew stronger Williamson became more paranoid and reclusive. Despite stamping his name across the city, from the hospitals to the public parks, he began to feel the deep resentment of some of the inhabitants, created by the repression of their liberty in work. In his final years, Lord Ashton completely distanced himself from a town that now felt alien to him.

It is usually the exploited who feel the alienation of place, but, in a perhaps distinctly northern way, Lancaster has shown in both its past and present the bonding of communities in the face of exploitation. While the ruins of Lancaster's port-town past may be steamrollered for new development and the dispute over Freeman's Wood rumbles on, it is heartening to see that their resistive spirit has not crumbled with the buildings.

Elizabeth Lee Reynolds

Storm and Steam

Portpatrick, Scotland

The last train vanished in a head of steam, leaving
a faint echo of its *rattle and clank, rattle
and clank*. Today tufts of coarse grass are waving

in the breeze: a ladybird lands on a nettle.
Shiny yachts dip and bob in a basin of water;
but where are the drovers and their horned cattle?

Where is the bride who embarked with her suitor?
The port was just a saint's stride from Ireland, but packets
went under, along with their cargoes. Better

times rarely crossed the horizon, but some pockets
jangled. Whispers were rife that smugglers frequented
sea-caves in which they would count out their ducats.

Only the moon saw feet that were planted
on boulders and ledges below Dunskey Castle: a piper
could sometimes be heard. Ring-netters mounted

the surf for herring, thanks to the skill of a trusty skipper.
Tempests claimed captains, whose names were chiselled
on stone in the kirkyard: how often was supper

eaten by women alone? The prevailing wind whistled
the names of wrecked vessels; *Lion, Fury,*
SS *Orion...* What became of drovers who jostled

livestock to safety? Their cattle would hurry
with horns interlocking and long tails swishing.
The steamers have gone, and these days a ferry

sails from Cairnryan. A high tide is washing
the yachts in their basin: gulls squawk and squabble
for pieces of batter. How many boats go fishing?

A Saltire flaps by the Dorn Rock anchor. The sea is stable
but rain is falling. Black Guillemots circle a plastic bottle,
then four red feet disappear in a bubble.

Who knows if the waves drown a *clank* and a *rattle*;
who knows if the wind...

Caroline Gill

Old World Trade and Modern Day Commerce

A Report from the Edge of the River

Every port is a trading post. It is the point at which compatibility is tested between a body of land, and the rest of the world. Bring us the products you have made, they say. Bring us your people. Bring us your past. And let us judge these things beside our own, that we might know if they clash or complement. Only then shall we know if the barrier should be raised – the barrier between us and you, between here and there, between our soil, and yours.

But it is an unruly, turbulent history, the history of negotiated exchange. Blood foams easily at the shoreline. And therein lurks the paradox of the port – instrument of enterprise, symbol of siege.

It was time to investigate. The city of Hull (technically Kingston upon Hull) seemed an appropriate location – sepia-postcard fishing town, new-world skyline, exits and entrances metaphorical and literal at the eastern edge of England. If ever a paradox might be found, it was here.

WALK #1: PRIORY SIDINGS

Woody Woodpecker – or his unanimated, less skilfully illustrated twin – keeps watch on the river for the return to Hull of its fishing fleet. He has been stationed on the defence wall near the place known as Priory Sidings, part of the former St Andrew's Dock – the dock that transported the product of the sea to the rest of the country, via the River Humber, from 1897 until the last fish train pulled away in 1965. About a hundred yards from the water's edge, I found the concrete railway platform from which cargo had been loaded and unloaded, hidden behind trees and bushes. Mounds of earth surrounded it. Other lost platforms survived elsewhere within that wayward undergrowth, insistently solid. Pathways had been trodden into the landscape, interlinking, rising, falling, venturing further inland through the uncontrolled vegetation toward the sizzle of traffic on the nearby A63, the main road in and out of Hull. Underfoot, the ground had been damaged by local kids racing motorbikes.

It was early when I arrived, the shingle on the foreshore not yet warm, and standing in that breaking light it was easy to imagine coming up on the horizon the mast of some spectral trawler finding its way back through time. I walked east, from where the trains no longer ran – bypassing, for now, the St Andrew's Quay Retail Park – to walk along the path beside the river, scattered with premium-strength beer cans, to where the filled-in former lock and its heavy gates wedged apart the land and the water, like the entrance to some Dark-Ages keep.

That stretch of outmoded coastline had been the farewell sight for hundreds of trawlermen. It would have been devoid of family (it was believed women present at the dock-side brought bad luck). Instead, they would say goodbye at the end of the terrace and walk to the river with their suitcases and their mates. They'd climb aboard and look back at their Yorkshire home as it gradually lost definition. Month after month. Year after year.

And then, after almost 100 years of maritime prosperity, demand renders the dock too small, and Iceland extends its fishing zone, and the war over cod is declared, and it all converges and by about 1975 the end of the fishing business in the city of Hull has truly begun.

They set out, present day forefathers, on their concluding journey. Once more to dredge the depths and never again. They bring up the last crowded net and hoist it over the side, and it swings aloft before the release and that customary yet somehow surprising gush. Looking down, they see the sun on the lens of a filmy fish-eye, the light split along its wet curve, the last of the miniature rainbows.

And so begins the inelegant dismantling of an industry, and during those years misfortune and disaster. Gas explosions. Unexplained drownings. A man pinned between vessel and timber, not a scream but a long groan, and after that only a subdued quiet, and a body raised up on ropes. The superstitious suggest a bony finger pointing from Reykjavik. Odd things turn up in nets: marine life on the wrong side of the globe, blood-red seaweed, the head of a dog packed in ice. Warnings from the north, they say. Or, in truth, they do not say, through fear that speaking the enchantment aloud might make it true.

Still, a hex on all our fleet. A hex on all our streets and houses. On all our families.

#

A blue plaque – circled with words of grief and love, flowers, poppies – has been put up at the former head of St Andrew's Dock.

Through these locks passed the ships and men who fished the Atlantic grounds of Murmansk, Greenland and Iceland. In 1914 and 1939 men and trawlers went to war. In peace and war this tablet commemorates the many who did not return.

To read the words, you must turn your back on dry land, and face the river.

WALK #2: CLARENCE FLOUR MILLS

The husk of a building on the bank of a different river – the river Hull, tributary of the Humber. Windows smashed, gates chained, perimeter patrolled by CCTV. Recently the site was added to the portfolio of Manor Properties, who intend to demolish and begin again. A 26-storey hotel and leisure complex. In the meantime, the obligatory razor-wire fence has been erected, and anyone foolish enough to step inside is reminded that their offence will always be prosecuted.

It was October, and I stood on the River Hull Boardwalk. On the opposite bank, several hundred feet off the ground, block lettering declared: CLARENCE FLOUR MILLS.

It hung above the city proudly. Over the decades it had absorbed fog, coal-smoke, petrol fumes.

As with any epic edifice it imposed itself best from a distance. It was boxy and sharp, barely a round angle in sight. It offered no apology for its interruption of sky. Somehow it seemed as if it had been raised from the earth, conjured overnight by inevitability and need, on the demand of progress, to stand one morning where a void had existed the evening before.

I crossed the river to be near the building. Only a few yards separated the old mill from the sheer drop to the brown tide, a deliberate architectural decision to enable wheat to be sucked into vast grain bins from the holds of barges. They moved a tonne every minute. It was a perfect geography discovered in the late 19th century by Joseph Rank (father of film mogul, J Arthur Rank), and faulted only in May 1941 when the mill was cracked open by the Luftwaffe and 15,000 tonnes of wheat slid into the river.

It was not possible to explore the inside of the mill without bolt cutters and a casual disregard for trespass. It had, however, been documented extensively online by urban explorers. Later, I watched footage, and wrote the following:

Wherever you stand in the abandoned mill you can hear the silence. It congregates at every station of the flour-making process: storage, grinding, warehousing, loading bay. If you walk and then stop its ferocity plunges about you unexpectedly, as if the engine had been unplugged only seconds before. It exhibits other noises which attend any large structure in demise. The distant slap of a tile dislodged by time from a toilet wall. A drop of falling water magnified through miles of unfilled corridor. The rustle of the mill's last surviving rat, a swollen bag of bones with a mad red in its one good eye, bunkered down inside some long-stopped machine like a Japanese solider guarding an outpost years after the rest of the world put away its guns. And in the stairwell, the banister is cold, when you touch it in the dark, your torch dancing sadly across the peeling walls, as you begin to climb...

#

INTERLUDE #1: PORT ENTREPRENEUR

Joseph Rank (1854–1943) first pulverizes grain into flour not by the side of the river but in a traditional windmill to the east of Hull. He starts young, works hard. Late 19th-century work ethic. Sacks of flour carried on his back to people's doorsteps. Dawn until midnight.

But the windmill fails to turn frequently enough. Rank stares at the sails one day, and wonders if he might cause them to rotate without the aid of nature. He installs a gas engine. Production increases, but only by a margin.

On a visit to Tadcaster, Rank is awed by a modern alternative. He borrows capital and builds his first mill, the Alexandra on Williamson Street: steel rollers, no millstones. The grinding is quicker, and ruin is held in abeyance, but profit still suffers a frustrating plateau due to the slow arrival of grain by cart. If he is to survive into the next century, he must mill much nearer the tide.

INTERLUDE #2: TIDAL ECONOMICS (OR, LOCATION IS NOT A MODERN CONCEPT)

He is a fool, Joseph Rank, or so his contemporaries claim. He has become obsessed by the river. He talks of buying land but not unless it falls within easy reach of the waterway. He speaks of a mill from which will emerge every 60 minutes an unprecedented 20 sacks of flour. The figures astound. A silo holding 20,000 quarters of grain. A 500bhp engine. Elevation at 40 tonnes per hour.

Despite the disbelief, they begin to build. Henry Simon of Manchester supply the roller mills. Belt-driven machines, intricate, operating on bronze bearings, housed in polished hardwood. Pulleys, jockey wheels. Six storeys of machinery. Grain in the back and flour out the front. Supply and demand in synchronicity.

The new world groans into life. The flour pours fast, the profit faster. The disparaging cry adjusts to applause. And the mill becomes a foremost enterprise in provincial England. Its owner is one of the wealthiest men in the north. Joseph Rank: Yorkshire Midas. Grain falling through fingers, turning to gold.

INTERLUDE #3: FEAR IN A HANDFUL OF YEAST

The idea on the riverbank lasts longer than a century before it is unable to abide by its founding principle. In

1962, the Rank Company buys Hovis-McDougall and Rank Hovis is formed. Further shuffles. Tomkins, Premier Foods. Continual change in the boardroom.

Up and down the country, mill workers no longer leave footprints on floury floors, but sit instead in computer rooms, tapping at consoles, analysing digital displays. At Hull prospective investors admire the beautiful but inefficient mechanics. In December 2005 they pull the plug. Everything judders and halts. The gate is dragged shut. In a nearby pub, with dusty white hands, the raising of a glass. To Joseph Rank and the Clarence Flour Mills, and to the kindness and the cruelty of technology.

#

WALK #3: ST. ANDREW'S QUAY RETAIL PARK

If you were to take a boat out on the Humber and look back toward land you might notice one of Hull's more popular retail parks glinting like paradise on the banks of the river. And if you took it upon yourself to row west toward Hessle, before circling back, you would see sliding along the shoreline zones of investment and zones of neglect, hauntingly juxtaposed. Drift east, in your hypothetical boat, away from the old railway lines, and the scenery fast-forwards half a century, from where an honest day's work earned an honest day's pay, to where the interest-free option gets around that loophole and newlyweds covet lampshades and sofas, and retailers reduce their names to marketable brands such as SCS, CSL and B&Q. A little work on the oar, and it's back to the obstinate past: the unhurried collapse of former dock buildings, a scattering of glass, the fire-damaged door behind which a shipping clerk once wrote studiously in a ledger.

When it was first conceived to pipe the water out of St Andrew's Dock and erect a retail and leisure complex, it was also decided that the youth of the city should put back into the local economy their respective contribution. Sadly, the ten-pin bowling alley and multiplex cinema did

not last long. The car park often flooded, the end lane at the Megabowl suffered an obvious camber, and the whole enterprise, some said, would slide into the silt before long, and leave behind the myth of modernity. Some said it

was as if the ground, unable to come to terms with being built upon, had given up on democracy and taken direct action by attempting to pull into itself every breezeblock put down in the name of commercial advance. And it had its supporters, the land that refused to accept milkshakes, French Fries and the CGI products of Armageddon-obsessed late 20th-century Hollywood. They lobbied to preserve. To turn back the diggers. To protect the past from free-market economics.

I do not know if their protest that day was caught on camera, if their solidarity perseveres in somebody's attic. But I feel I can see them, today, as I stand against the wind. The few, the faithful, benevolently prejudiced few, stamping their feet in the cold and the spray off the river. I imagine they had their hands in their raincoat pockets. I imagine their collars would have been turned up, their eyes cast sadly down to where the ground was to be broken by a local actor or proud dignitary.

Like that they were, I think. Like that.

#

We build to an agenda, that's the thing. We build where the bankers want us to build. They exploit our love of empire, or the love of empire they think we have. And they have us believe that the unconstructed future is everything we need, and that it will boom, and feel good, like the past.

#

AT THE HEART OF THE PARADOX

Maritime relics protrude from the river-bed, even now, as if the previous century left behind its carcass. Dockside remains fall reluctantly into sediment. With their sturdy construction they seem embarrassed of the thing they have become — confused, desperate tangles of iron and timber. But not far behind the rot and the rust, ferries bring freight from mainland Europe to the doors of the kingdom. They part the same waters into which the past abandons itself. And their passage is slow, as if in respect.

This is the contradiction that is Hull. It is a contradiction founded on geography. Its estuarine location is an irony often overlooked: the river as lifeblood, the river as executioner.

It is the contradiction of the port – trading post, place of power, paradox.

Jason Gould

North Pier, Oban

The warmest February day ever recorded in Scotland

Usually, people aren't this happy.
Usually, people aren't this dry.

No Naked Lights.
During lifting operations
all hatches must be closed.
Adgang Forbrudt.

Two boys skim stones,
two fathers approve.
An old couple on a bench
compare the day with Spain.

Isolate at source before opening.
No caravans.
No more than 7 degrees must be obtained
when lifting.

Men in red hats and yellow trousers lay tarmac.
It takes 8.
Men in white hats and blue trousers
inspect The Havagull. It takes 4.

Please don't stand or sit on the wall.
Keep walkway clear of equipment.
Hats and boots must be worn at all times.

Someone is fully certificated
Someone is fully registered.
Someone has the right licence.
Someone is under the max gross weight.

No pedestrian access.
Shut off in the event of unauthorised access.

Usually, people aren't posing for photos.
Usually, people aren't looking at the Ronja Skye,
registered in Alesund.

Queue here for seal colony.
Reserved for Search and Rescue.
Queue here for mermaid colony.

Someone is listening to rumours
of illegal scallop dredging.
A centurion lock hangs on an orange container.
Gulls arrogantly hang around a gantry.
Take care on the pontoons.

Out on the pontoons,
the buoyant lifeboaters are practising:
how to save somebody from becoming some body.
Be Aware!

Someone floats in a white hat,
shouting to be rescued.
The blue hats swim out, pull ropes.
It takes 5.

The green hats run around
mimicking urgency.
Be aware!
People change hats
and do it all again.

Can be slippery.
Don't dare!

Someone jumps from pontoon to pontoon.
Someone leaps into the sweet sea
for no obvious reason but the sunshine.
The boys are still skimming stones.

Please don't stand or kneel on these benches.
This is not a step.

For the first time I see a link
between the words "levity" and "levitation".
Someone, somewhere,
has removed the sign saying *No Laughing*.

Seth Crook

Hard to see the harbour from the harbour road. Hard to think of harbours without the visible impact of humans. What is this port or harbour? How crumbling buildings gradually give up their secrets, or hold out for a freshly painted sign. Mere fortifications against a tide. Here, instead, soft channels and scrapes of earth. A whimbrel's bill, a buddleia's arc, a castaway pebble that stitches the hem of sea. Air like milk and chiffon where a summer wind sweeps up the light dust of brick across a mirage of ground. Out to a kind of port held in reserve for nature, it's arrival, departures, everything in passage, a re-wilded desert aggregated with brittle ghosts, pebble, soil, concrete and sand, where progress occurs with the slightest of touches, with sea kale and campion, each in turn. The faces of tourists, naturalists, dog walkers, all in some ways orphaned by the sea, the salt-caked stones, outliers out with the pioneer plants, transfixed for a ruderal hour, seeing nothing but what might be lost, what might be won.

Container City

Ports and criminality is an old story. Every port in every city that has ever existed has this kind of problem. Ports are a gateway, an entry point or transit point, for many different things.

The illicit trafficking that goes through UK ports, like anywhere, follows the established routes of legal trade. Illegal goods, including drugs, can arrive in bulk via container ports. Some drugs are particularly suitable for container shipping. While passenger ships are used to ship small quantities within vehicles or luggage, with or without a passenger knowing, within containers you can ship kilos and kilos of cocaine or heroin.

An individual passenger might only to bring in one or two kilos, and there are much tighter controls on passengers – so the risk is higher. But if you send five containers on a ship with 100 kilos of cocaine in each, and you manage to stop one container, then there's still 400 kilos of cocaine coming into the country. A network of criminals will know that some of it will get checked and stopped. It's a matter of economic scale and a risk you factor in.

Felixstowe and Liverpool are currently the UK's two largest container ports, but they are very different because of where they are located. Liverpool is on the Atlantic route, and that means connections to North America – Montreal, Halifax, New York and the eastern seaboard. Liverpool also has deeper water than other UK ports, which makes it the best choice for the largest container ships – including some of a size that other ports can't host. A lot of Felixtowe's trade comes via Europe, from Rotterdam and Antwerp – the biggest ports in Europe.

Drugs come by different routes too. With cocaine, you're talking about Latin America, so Liverpool might be the port of choice. With heroin, it comes from Asia and across Europe by road or air, and then into the UK via a seaport or airport. So heroin arrives by the European shipping routes.

Even with legal cargoes, port economies are still extremely tied up with geographical space.

When it comes to organised crime, you also need to look at the city behind the port itself. In the UK, Liverpool has always had a particular space in the history of organised crime, and there has been an aura of independence about the gangs there that the rest of the country didn't have. It has run through families and across generations and become entrenched in the city economy and developed strong direct links with narco-traffickers in Latin America. These gangs may not always ship things directly to Liverpool, they use other ports as well.

This can't be said of Felixstowe, which doesn't have a city behind it. Felixstowe is used on a more opportunistic basis by Dutch groups, Italian groups and other European groups that want to ship things to the UK. In some ways it's a little bit more chaotic, whereas if you want to ship to Liverpool you need to have a good understanding of how organised crime works in the city.

The supply chain for something like cocaine can be very complex. If you sell drugs as a local distributor across Merseyside and you know you have a pool of buyers, you might decide you need 100 kilos of the drug every six months. First, you need to connect with your own personal networks, maybe to a Dutch or Albanian 'high distributor' group based in the city. These operate as brokers, and will tell you that they know someone in Colombia or Panama that can get you that amount of cocaine. These brokers may also be based in Italy or Holland, say, but be servicing Merseyside.

The brokers put your request to the traffickers, who may be based somewhere else again – Colombia, or Peru, perhaps. You will have no idea who or where they are. Then at some point you will receive a call from someone, who again you may not know, who will tell you that in a week's time at a certain dock, in container A, B or C, shipped by company X, coming from a particular country, at a particular hour, you will find 50 kilos of the total shipment. You have no idea how it got there, but you know it's yours. You receive shipments like this on a rolling basis as instalments of the full amount.

Getting illicit cargo into containers used to work by what was called the 'ripping off system'. This involved having someone at the port in Peru or Mexico or wherever, who could place bags of cocaine into a container that is full of, say, computer printers, without the authorities knowing. The person asking for the container of printers to be sent doesn't know it will also contain drugs, and the ship's owners don't know either. Both have been 'ripped off'. The container gets loaded up with the legal cargo first, and then someone comes at night, opens up the container, puts the drugs at the front, and then closes it as if nothing has happened.

When the container arrives at its destination, the broker sends someone to open it up as it arrives. This is a complex operation, due to the amount of containers that come through a big port. You need access and a plan of the port, and to be able to locate the container, open it, take out the drugs and close it again. Links between organised crime groups and port workers means there will be people there who can make this happen. A port is a gated community, and it often takes on the typical dynamics of one. It's also a quintessential example of a working-class community that might want to go against authority, and it's usually an almost totally masculine environment, too.

However, getting drugs out of ports has become more difficult as security systems have improved. So what has happened is that trafficking has started to occur with the participation of the freight forwarder or the people asking for the legal shipment, by hiding the drugs within a legitimate cargo. This however, requires more sophistication from the organised crime group by creating fake orders and shipments.

Remember that maybe only five per cent of containers are checked. If there is specific intelligence that a container might contain illicit goods, then police will have the authority to open it, but random checks don't really happen. It's like a giant postal service – and you don't have random searches opening up your envelopes and mail to check what's inside.

However, there are always ways round security systems. If you study them, you will find their vulnerabilities. If there is corruption within the Border Force, then that's another problem.

If you are in organised crime but don't have a poly-crime agenda and only want to ship drugs for a limited period, then to get drugs out of the port all you really need is a contact within the port – a port employee. All UK ports are privately owned and on private land, so the employee could be in the private port police, or in the Border Force, or even a crane operator.

Other groups want to stay out of the drugs market but stay in the port, so they might offer protection, asking a fee to provide a safe journey to people who want to ship certain cargoes. The people that do this usually want to stay in a city, be active outside the port, and build their reputation. Or you might want to gain control of part of a port's economy, infiltrating the port by bidding for contracts to provide cranes, for example. That also takes your people inside the port to work in semi-legal ways.

Remember, ports are a point of transit, not a gate. They are about logistics and transport systems. This raises questions of governance and high-level, white-collar corruption. The global port economy is led by only six major companies around the world – including MSC, the global cruise and shipping line registered in Switzerland, which owns many of the ports in Europe, and Maersk, the Danish container shipping company. The total global port economy is governed by this handful of big players… but that's another story altogether.

Dr Anna Sergi

Locating   /   /
low-density housing / first then di-
visions / between old and new / the
vegetated shingle spit

designated as
common land /
land withstand-
ing exposure /
to salt spray /
perhaps erosion
or / burial

beyond boatyard /and the phrases /
beach-shacky / the convoy of articulated
lorries

or a guide /
post-****** /
supply-chain
reliability
/ conges-
tion-free
short sea
sailing routes

then definitions: shingle sediment
/ of certain particle size / range of
2–200mm /

lowland acid / enriched soils / coarser
grasses / not letting sward / become
rank / on unimproved pasture

Dune waxcap / early forget-me-not /
common storksbill / reserve rabbits / sea
kale (crambe maritima)

the plover in decline / the whelk
eggs / purse for mermaid / sea
slater and kelp

by rifle butts / and tank trap / barrack
/ searchlight / gun emplacement / the
divided sedge and grass vetchling

the bastion view-
point / some for-
tification / against
seaborne invasion
/ the ringing
studies / the moth
traps / the lichen
still to come

Musings on Lower East Street

Mustard love heart, sharp left;
scrapyard, hunks of pre-owned
metal, riverside, seven deep –

balanced, it should be like this,
trucks, cables, a Cadillac trunk,
something is invariably rusting,

it's a gritty day, September and
Nile Greens smart on a mattress,
naturally violated pastellic foam,

cobra conduit, crude, shotcrete,
ferrocement, double bitt, fetch,
an uninhibited mobile wedge of

warmest possibility, nearest to a
shady brutalistic port on a cool
afternoon, steady progress of a

dredger, casual pyramids, Pebble
Rover, Bore Song and one silent
Sunday sunflower by the stillest

ambulance, coupled, wayside,
tipped, tobacco ditch, on call for
Autumn, ready to rescue Summer.

Julie Hogg

Ocean Horizon

I trained in the late 1980s as an electrical engineer in communist Romania. I was working in a factory and had strong working ties with the workers. After communism collapsed in 1989, many of them became unemployed and tried to find a job in Europe. During this period I changed my professional life by studying painting at the Arts Academy in Iasi, Romania in the early 1990s.

As an artist, one of my main interests is the exploration of the social practices in arts and the ethics of representation in order to map the dramatic changes in post-communist Romania and Eastern Europe. My work primarily focuses on documentary format research in photography and film and on the way these mediums can redefine the notions of truth (evidence) and singularity (poetics).

I made *Maersk Dubai* and *Travel Guide* in the mid-2000s around the time of the admission of Romania into the EU. Both works describe the difficult 1990s, when the Romanians couldn't travel and work. This situation left many people unemployed and desperate to find a job. Both of these projects explore the precarious and risky conditions Romanian illegal workers faced in Europe during that time.

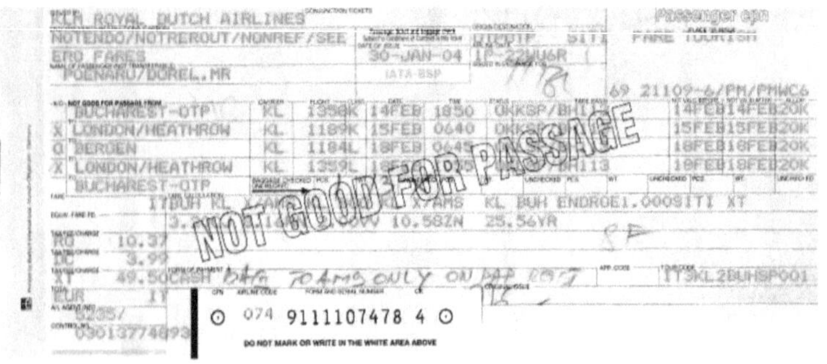

Travel Guide was produced in 2005 and is a comprehensive set of instructions and documents for Romanian illegal workers on how to get to UK without a visa. I met several illegal workers and recorded their stories. I carried out internet research on the subject before

Fig.6 Containers shipping in the ferry-boats in Le Havre

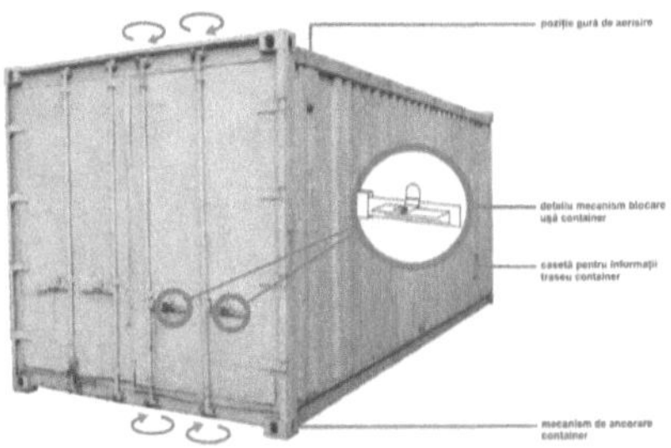

Fig.7 Locking mechanism of the containers

assembling a wealth of anecdotal and written information, and brought them together in the format of a commerical travel guide. The original format for *Travel Guide* was a leaflet distributed free in the exhibition space. The guide describes in detail a wide range of routes into the EU. It advises on accomodation while making your way to the various ports and airports, and about obtaining an EU passport. It also talks you through the perilous process of entering England without a visa if you get a plane ticket with a stop at Heathrow Airport, what to wear at ports to avoid suspicion and the dangerous practice of sneaking into – and finding air pockets in – shipping containers.

For the gallery space I decided to include a vinyl map on the wall or on the floor, together with the leaflets, in order to make the viewer's experience more powerful, both visually and mentally. I think maps always encourage our imagination. I had an interesting reaction when presenting *Travel Guide* in Vienna. The EU Culture

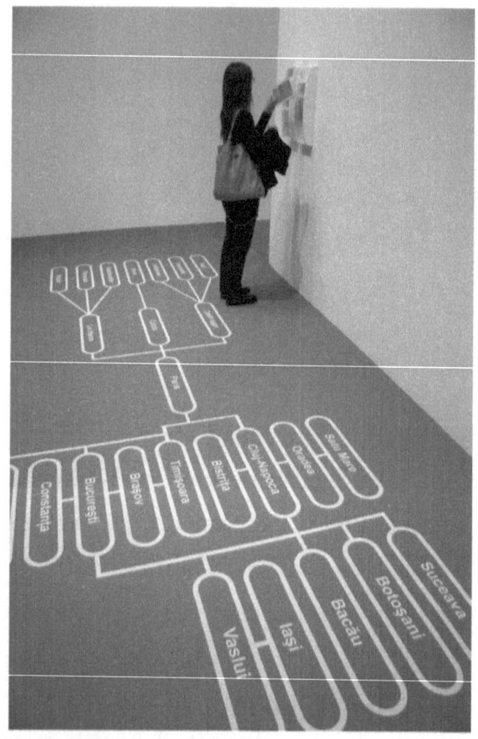

Travel Guide, installation, *The Irresistible Force*, Tate Modern, 2007

Commissioner saw the piece and I think he felt embarrassed by the subversive dimension of my work.

The video *Maersk Dubai* from 2007 tells the story of the murder of three Romanians who had illegally embarked on a ferry for the destination of Halifax, Canada. The Romanians were discovered by the Taiwanese captain, who ordered to throw them into the Atlantic Ocean. I was deeply affected by their tragic death; a symbol for the tragedy of my country at that time.

I am very much committed to photography and film, that's why many of my projects take shape in these mediums. For *Maersk Dubai*, the backbone of the film was the commentary; not only the sad story of the murders, but also the deep and abysmal experience of thinking about dying a death that couldn't happen in a fraction of a second. What are you thinking and doing with your life when you know that your days, or even hours, are numbered? The leitmotif is the ocean horizon, which I filmed several times with the idea of encouraging the viewer to meditate.

The *Maersk Dubai* piece affected some people who saw the video. I had many emotional conversations with visitors to the galleries or museums where the piece was exhibited.

In both works I wanted to raise awareness of the condition of the people who felt the need to undertake such an uncertain journey. Most of these people were suffering after the fall of communism. I understood better after making these works that I love people in general because I don't have close friends. Many of the emotions and ideas from these projects are my projections and visions about the world. They are like my conceptual self-portrait.

Matei Bejenaru

Poplars, the otherside of the narrow channel of water known as The Haven. Scalp Road crumbling into the churned earth of arable land. Everything wide and open, haw and blackthorn huddling at low perimeters. An upended traffic cone near a gateless turning into a field. The field bare. And then the road turns inland through a smattering of dwellings, giving brief views of industry, into Fishtoft, Scrane End, Tamworth Green, and more channels – The Graft, Hobhole Drain. The River Witham becomes The Haven, passing a succession of bridges, locks, docks and drains on its way to sea. The Witham Navigable Drains, part of a 438-mile drainage system that crosses the Lincolnshire fenland, including South Forty-Foot Drain, or the Black Sluice Navigation. These are tidal lands, lands of creeks and saltmarshes, from where the Scrooby pilgrims left – first for Holland, then on to America. The Haven, part of the Port of Boston, draws shipping up from The Wash and the Boston Deeps, into Boston itself. From here wool once left for Flanders. Now it's scrap steel, paper, grain, timber and ubiquitous containers, lifted by cranes in a Victorian port, a port still at work, inland looking out.

Boutique by the Harbour

Inscrutable
save for the moments
when shadows
flick the cheekbones
or breezes
tease the eyelids

seeing nothing
she watches everything,
the harbour
and ships
and breezes
that carry a man away.

In the fashion posh-shop
she stands daily
at the window,
dressed to sell,
the mannequin
with the languid look.

And behind the counter
on a low-season day
Crista checks her messages
one more time.

Charlie Lambert

DETENTION PORTS

SUBJECT TO CLARIFICATION:

Detention for immigration purposes is an administrative and not a criminal process. There are none of the safeguards that there should be when depriving someone of their liberty. The decision to detain an individual is taken by an immigration officer and not overseen by a court. Subsequent decisions to maintain detention are also not subject to independent judicial oversight. After being released people can be re-detained at any point without warning. Sometimes people are detained while reporting to the Home Office (thus demonstrating compliance with their conditions) and others are forcibly removed from their homes in a raid.

The UK is the only country in Europe without a time limit on immigration detention.
• 24,748 individuals entered detention in 2018.
• There are 3,500 bed spaces for people to be detained under immigration powers, including 400 spaces in HM prisons.
• Anyone subject to immigration control can be detained.

There is well established common law, known as the 'Hardial Singh' principles, which set out limits on the lawful use of detention:

1. The Secretary of State must intend to deport the person and can
only use the power to detain for that purpose;

2. The deportee may only be detained for a period that is
reasonable in all the circumstances;

3. If, before the expiry of the reasonable period, it becomes
apparent that the Secretary of State will not be able to effect
deportation within a reasonable period, he should not seek to
exercise the power of detention;

4. The Secretary of State should act with all diligence and
expedition to effect removal.

143 DAYS

Average length of time detained asylum seekers are held.
Vulnerable adults, including survivors of torture or trafficking, or
people with severe mental health issues or learning difficulties are
regularly detained for long periods.

*"They will shout at you and think you're a piece of shit, because
you've got immigration issues they'll just treat us wrong. That
goes for some of the staff – probably the majority are like that."*

The Home Office's casual attitude to liberty is encapsulated by
its frequent refusal to allocate Asylum Support accommodation
to detainees to enable them to apply for bail on the grounds that:

"applicants housed in detention are not destitute by the fact that they are being housed and their dietary needs are catered to. Detention is based around shared facilities (bedrooms, shower rooms & dining rooms) which is not too dissimilar to emergency accommodation with lack of liberty being the main difference".

'THE BLOCK'

The Block is a site of solitary confinement within an Immigration Removal Centre. Officially, it is called the Care and Separation Unit (CSU). The CSU is intended to be a last resort measure for protecting the safety and security of the segregated individual as well as all other detainees.

The Home Office's guidance on these units states that "its use must be necessary" and "all other options [should] be exhausted." While in segregation, detainees are most often locked up in their cells for 23 hours per day without access to IRC facilities. Each year, between 1,200 to 4,800 detainees are placed in segregation units in IRCs in the UK.

"I was in my room sleeping, during bang-up time, and they came and told me that they had to move me to CSU. It was without explanation. They've been doing it when they arrested me from my house. They refused to explain why. I didn't fight or argue with them - they wanted to handcuff me, and I said why are you doing that? I said no, I'm not

having handcuffs on my hand. I was complying. They were videoing me at the same time, I said 'why are you videoing me' and they said it's part of the procedure. I asked for a copy of the video, and they said I have to ask my solicitor. When I got there they explained it's because they'd had a call from immigration, who said they had a travel document and a deportation had been authorized and I had a flight on the 31st. One officer told me that it is normally only a day before the flight that you get moved to the CSU (the block). He said it was the first time that they'd done it like this he'd never seen someone be moved to the block a week before their flight. My ticket has been cancelled and they're saying that once they get confirmation of it they will move me back to the unit."

Violence is common within detention. Individuals are locked in confined spaces with people that they do not know, many of whom are acutely vulnerable, alienated from society at large and facing an uncertain length of detention and the threat of potential removal from the country. Issues of violence are exacerbated by endemic staff shortages. Processes to remove people on charter flights are understood to be particularly brutal and intimidating, with reports of people being restrained even when there is no reason to do so.

"'I can't breathe.' They didn't care."

The stated purpose of the Home Office's Adults at Risk (AAR) policy, introduced in 2016, was to reduce the number of vulnerable people being detained.

Following the introduction of the Adults at Risk policy, vulnerable people now have to show that they are being harmed by detention instead of the Home Office taking a preventative approach to ensure that harm is not done.

For example, rather than not detaining a torture survivor simply because they have been identified as a torture survivor (and there is therefore an increased likelihood that they could be vulnerable due to their past experiences), the Home Office now requires evidence that there is a significant risk of harm to that particular individual. In practice, this usually means producing evidence of a deterioration in their mental or physical health, i.e. that harm has already been done.

RECOMMENDATION 8:

A time limit of 28 days for all should be introduced to reduce the overall harm of detention on all people detained and a shorter seven-day statutory time limit should be enacted for those identified as Adults at Risk.

*   *   *

Do you want to get out of detention, but don't know how?
DISCLAIMER: The following information is updated regularly and
is, to the best of our knowledge, correct at the time of writing.
However, immigration law changes frequently and it is advisable
to check with a solicitor or qualified immigration advisor that the
advice given in this book is up to date and relevant.

*WE HAVE TRIED TO AVOID USING WORDS WHICH ARE
DIFFICULT TO UNDERSTAND.*

GENERAL ADVICE ON HOW BEST TO REPRESENT YOURSELF

1. Make sure you keep all documents that are sent to you by the
Home Office, or by your legal representative. You may be tempted
to destroy documents which seem unimportant to you. DO NOT
DESTROY OR THROW AWAY ANY DOCUMENTS.

However unimportant a document may seem, it could be important
to your case. Keep any refusals of bail, bail summaries, or letters from
the Home Office relating to your case. If you go to see a solicitor or
advisor, take your documents with you, so that you can show them to
the advisor.

2. If you fax the Home Office, make sure that you keep a copy of the
letter and the fax receipt which shows that your letter was sent.
Fax receipts can be kept as evidence that you have written to the Home
Office. It is their duty to respond to you if you contact them. If you can

prove that they have not replied, it could help you with your case.
3. Try to remain polite at all times to removal centre staff, Home
Office officials and immigration judges.

You may believe that you are being badly treated. You may also
feel a sense of anger and frustration at your situation. However, if you
behave in a way which is considered rude or aggressive, this may
be used against you as an argument to keep you detained. Don't
give officials a reason to make your life more difficult. If you have
complaints, put them politely in writing, or use the IMB (Independent
Monitoring Board) boxes in detention centres to complain.
4. Write to your caseworker to find out about the progress of your
case. This will not only keep you informed, but will also show the
court that you are taking steps to progress your case. This could
help you to get released.

FREQUENTLY ASKED QUESTIONS
What am I doing here?
There is a good chance that either you, or somebody you know, is
in immigration detention. You want to know what to do next.
What is immigration detention?
Detention centres are used by the UK government to place people
who they believe do not have a legal right to stay in the UK, or
whose legal right to be here is being decided, while they try to

remove or deport them. Some prisons are also used.

Why am I in detention?

The reasons for your detention may vary.

What is the point of detention?

This is a good question.

How long do I have to stay here?

There is no time limit on immigration detention.

The Ramsgate Ferryman

These northern Waters, cold and unforgiving, crash
against the broken shore beneath his Island feet.
A sfumato statue – lost or still emerging
from the snorting breath of bulls (four score and nine) – he
tugs his mantle. Pebbles rattle, like knucklebones.

If doubts were birds his skies are silent. All he hears
is that clamour of the Strait and this incessant
whispering of Sand. Patient as Penelope
he waits. *What news?* (A Play of Ignorance.) Harried
schemer, wishful weaver, his whole cloth unravels

even as it leaves the Loom. This barest of threads -
Ware Atropos! – his Suitors, the yet-living dead,
the Counted Ones, draw close enough to hear his con-
fidence, that he Believes, and so is rewarded.
All his obols, treasures hoarded – *that Croesus had*

such care! – have been, with purpose true, and pleasure spent
most diligently. But still the Banks sit empty.
Might this be Fate? Close, and closer, his foam-flecked Suit-
ors crowd, turbid eyes beseech The Day's arrival,
yet see no more than this – blameless – misnamed Charon.

For there are no Ferries arriving at the dock,
nor any Sign, upon the waves, of sea borne freight.

RG Jodah

In Search of the Port of Manchester

We've just been to the Isle of Man for a long weekend. With a little under 100 miles of coastline to explore, ports became the recurring motif of our visit. Small and appearing from a jumble of streets, they sat under a postcard-blue sky as ports should, some at low water with boats tipped sideways on the bottom, others filled with sparkling calmness. There were gulls, tea shops, and nearby beaches marked with a high tide of seaweed. If I were to draw a port from memory, any one of them could have provided the template. The concept of a port which stretches for many miles along an inland waterway is one I'm still getting my head round, and something I'd spent the previous few weeks exploring. We'd seen it, part of it, the port which had brought this question into my mind in the first place, as we flew out from Manchester on our way to Man.

The Port of Manchester is 36 miles long, the main length of it passing through Salford and Warrington, Cheshire and the Wirral with only the tiniest section actually reaching Manchester. I say port, but there's no actual 'port' for you to go and stand in, or next to, or across from. It's idea rather than destination, simultaneously the Manchester Ship Canal and not the Ship Canal. Its owners, the Peel Ports Group, explain how the Ship Canal 'spearheaded deep-sea shipping to the heart of Manchester (making) the city's port the third busiest in Britain.' You'd read that and think that the port was a separate entity from the canal, wouldn't you? Especially when Wikipedia chimes in with the information that the port was created before the opening of the canal. But the canal is the port, though you certainly couldn't say that the port was the canal. The port is the length of the canal, the canal forms the port, and neither are really in Manchester at all. I need to go out there and find it.

The trouble is, I'm not sure where to start.

ONE: POMONA DOCKS TO SALFORD QUAYS

This part is at least familiar. We've walked out to the Quays this way before, though I hadn't grasped then how the Ship Canal was connected to the Irwell. I think of the Irwell as a Manchester river, but that's stretching things really. It only skirts the city for a short distance, curving down through Salford to make a boundary, and all the riverside paths and love are on the Salford side. All rivers belong to more than one place, of course, with tributaries rising in one place, building into streams, adding their contribution to a wider flow which passes where it pleases on its way to the sea. Rivers were there first, with settlements growing around them. Canals work the other way.

Manchester wanted its route to the sea, and the plan began with the Irwell. The Ship Canal's architects took the Irwell where it made its way out of Manchester and turned it into the start of their navigation. I reckon this is about where the Germanically-named Woden Street Bridge crosses from the Castlefield area. Mythology is blended here as much as the water from river to canal: I'm looking across at what was once Pomona Docks, the final calling point for boats. Pomona was the Roman goddess of fruitfulness, and the land wedged here between the parallel lines of the Bridgewater canal and the Irwell/Ship Canal was once Manchester's pleasure gardens. It's now optimistically designated as one of a series of River Parks, though the only sign of this regeneration is a relatively modest set of apartment buildings, flanked by waiting derelict land. There's a tall, narrow information board on the river path with a guide to walking represented in the manner of a Tube route. Its straight blue line passes through the 'zones' of the different River Parks, with tram links and places of interest making up the 'stations'. The point at which the Irwell becomes the Ship Canal, nature becoming industry, isn't interesting enough to be on there. No-one's reading it, anyway. On this beautiful, sunny day, the only other person around is a solitary graffiti artist.

Graffiti is a bit of a theme on all urban canals, but particularly here. I watch the artist at work for a moment. Does it still count as graffiti if you're doing it on a semi-designated wall in broad daylight and full view? It doesn't seem transgressive enough, even though he has a bag of Red Stripe lager by his feet. Further along, I start taking photos of the squat, low bollards, left from the time when ships needed to be tied up along here. Each one has been decorated with a swirling coat of colour, the squiggles and tags overlapping in bursts of exuberance. They feel like anarchic cousins to the corporate art trails that sprang up in many cities last summer. Manchester had bees – four-foot-high identical models which various artists were commissioned to decorate. The results were fun, a controlled art project with maps and apps you could follow around the city, tracking Manchester's 'architectural, industrial and cultural heritage.' Those bees have been sold off now, for fairly large sums. There weren't any put here, though. Fear of them ending up in the water? Health and safety concerns about people falling in? It illustrates the disconnect between the actual heritage here and the footfall tracking it down.

It's very different in Salford Quays, where the regeneration happened a generation ago. On a map, the quays make the shape of a clawed hand. It's one of the area's most recognisable features, and the Quays themselves are a symbol of the new Manchester: media city and cultural hub, a phoenix of regeneration. Architects have outdone each other to design iconic buildings, with odd bits sticking out of dramatic facades, an oil drum barbecue resting above the entrance of the Lowry theatre and art gallery, a shard piercing the roof of the war museum. Bronze glass, gold glass, a sense of Art Deco. Media is the new industry. There's still a sense of impermanence, though – something that went up so (relatively) fast could all be pulled down, and the docks reinstated in some future post-media dystopia. Utopia? In the final dock, the only one connected to the rest of the Ship Canal, a barge is clearing storm detritus. The vegetation forms a carpet, almost rigid enough to walk on. The barge sits in the middle of it, its single grasping bucket reaching for handful after dripping handful which are swung around to be dumped into the hold behind. It's a Sisyphean task. I watch for a long time, wondering just how long it'll take to get down to clear water. There are no other boats, no arrivals here by water except this wind-blown, unwanted debris.

TWO: PORT OF SALFORD TO IRLAM LOCKS

I'm still trying to get my head around where the Port of Manchester is. Whilst I'm looking around online, I come across a mention of the Port of Salford, and this port has a postcode. I have an afternoon to spare and the map says it's a half hour drive away, beyond Trafford Park (the world's first planned industrial estate) and Barton swing bridge (the only swing aqueduct in the world), which carries the Bridgewater Canal (the UK's first manmade canal) across the Ship Canal. We also go past City Airport, previously Barton Aerodrome (and the UK's first purpose-built municipal airport. Are you getting the theme here?). None of it makes much of a splash. I drive past, on the suburban roads of the Greater Manchester of semi-detached, post-war houses, chain pubs and supermarkets. Then there's one of those in-between areas of blankness. The road is now a dual carriageway, with nowhere to stop. The Ship Canal is over to the left somewhere but it might as well not be there. That's something else rivers and canals have in common – the ability to disappear until you're right next to them. I've watched YouTube videos of ships coming along the canal, vast superstructures gliding through the fields like a cut-out picture on a lolly stick. It would be cool to see them today, keeping pace with the cars on this road. The sight might make me crash, mind.

I'm not sure what I'm expecting of the port, but it's probably more than a vast, impersonal warehouse. I am expecting to see something connected to the water. From what I've read, which is entirely promotional guff, Port Salford will one day be the UK's first tri-modal inland waterway port, served by ship, rail and road and currently fully operational. It's a ground breaking development which will include an inland port and warehousing facility, a container terminal and a distribution park. So far, just the road and rail links are operational. This is a port without a port, without a dock, or a connection to water or even a view of water. I drive along Port Salford Way, which leads to a huge warehouse, with a blank front and no visible entrance. Every so often, a lorry goes by, disappearing around to the back. It's possible that the port is back there, I suppose, but there's no way through for a casual visitor. I turn around and drive back out, pulling in to a space which specifies no parking. Maybe there's a viewline down to the water from this angle. Nothing.

I feel a need to see the canal, to verify its existence. The dual carriageway takes me backwards and forwards, but there's nowhere to stop. Finally, about a mile along, I come across a small, new housing estate on the far side of the road and hope that there aren't resident-only restrictions.

Back across the roads, dodging the warehouse-bound lorries, we finally find an entrance and, beyond that, not only the canal but a complex of locks. There are gates, but one is standing open and a Peel Holdings van is parked inside. The whole air is of dereliction, with two old guys in hi-vis PPE working on some non-specific maintenance. They ignore us. Working on the basis that they'll tell us as soon as we go too far, I step into the yard and peer through the wire fencing. The men continue ignore me, but in that way that says they won't be welcoming any questions. All that's visible is lines of metal, attached to stretches of concrete. We see a tiny footpath, literally shoulders-width, heading off in parallel with where the river must be. It takes us along by the locks, a 1980s housing block on the other side. It's in a weird position, itself squashed between main road and an industrial yard. I'm just wondering if it was sold on the premise of classy waterside living when a runner squeezes past and disappears off to one side. It's like a magic trick, because she appears to melt through the metal barrier. We go back to see how she did it, and realise the footpath actually has access to a metal bridge crossing over the canal.

From the middle, peering through a mesh that's too closely formed to allow for photos, we look out at this industrial remnant of a system designed to move huge ships along a man-made channel to a landlocked city. They're very different to the locks you find on smaller canals. Those have an air of history, with waist-high wooden beams, hand-painted in black with white edging. They cross the line into rural heritage, a charming reminder of a past time, to be used today for slow-time leisure. No-one would come to see these for their charm. There are more men there, in orange overalls, a reminder that these locks, despite their air of desolation, are still operational. As we cross over and walk along a small road, I keep having to remind myself of this. The Port of Salford is a mile along, with its plans of a tri-modal future. Here is all peace and emptiness. The tiny track, a robin. Over the hedge are stables, then a water treatment plant. The canal is river-like here, with uneven edges, a cormorant fishing from the bank. There's a wholly derelict structure, remains of a wooden quayside, jutting out into the water. It's impossible to work out what it was for.

On the way back, we go past a couple of other Peel Holdings guys who are sitting in their van having a chat. They are more approachable, and I stop to pepper them with questions. Yes, boats still go through here. There was one only yesterday, and there were usually two or three a week. I could find a marine app online to see when the next one would be, or wait until the summer season and watch the ferry trip boat come along from Liverpool. The abandoned quay on the other side of the lock turns out to be the landing stage for boats connecting with the sewage works. I forget to ask which way their exchange goes bringing waste or collecting fertiliser – but it reminds me of the old guys on the Leeds/Liverpool canal where I live, reminiscing about the boats bringing night soil from Liverpool to spread on the fields.

I ask them about Port Salford and they haven't got a clue what I mean. Along there, I say, pointing up river. Salford Quays? One of them asks. He looks puzzled. The boats don't go there anymore. No, I say, the distribution place. The other guy chips in and they both nod. You get a lot of lorries, they say. I ask if they see the canal picking up again, ships coming through? Yes, there is a plan for a new port there. No, they weren't expecting it to happen any day soon. I ask if there's anywhere else you can walk along the Ship Canal and he suggests, after a bit of thought, Latchford Locks near Warrington. Later, I try to log on to a marine site to find out when a ship is next going through. The information is hidden unless I get a paid subscription. I watch more YouTube videos instead, of huge ships sliding through fields.

THREE: THELWALL

The viaduct is a long line ahead of us, just visible over a clump of trees. We walk through empty fields to reach a track fringed with hawthorn and early bramble growth, the river just a glimpse beyond. It's absolutely quiet here, other than the roar of cars from the M6 ahead. It's a sound that will be with us all day. Soon we're under the motorway, in a hidden world. I've passed overhead countless numbers of times, driving south or on a trip to IKEA in Warrington. You don't have time on the motorway to stop and look at the passing scenery, though. In a photo I took underneath the viaduct, there's grass and sky in one half, and dozens of grey concrete columns in the other. I look at the picture and try to count them: there must be 50 altogether on that side of the canal. From this angle I took the photo from, you can't see any traffic and in the photo there is, of course, no sound. The road seems abandoned, a relic of another time. A glimpse of a future without cars? Who knows? It would be no different to a ship canal without ships, and I've not seen a single one of those.

It takes us about 20 minutes to reach the Thelwall ferry. This comprises a tiny wooden dock next to a tidy patch of green lawn. Tied to a white-painted fence is an aluminium rowing boat, big enough for maybe four passengers at a time. A board nearby tells us that a crossing costs 11p, and runs daily between 7am and 9am, 12pm and 2pm, 4pm and 6pm. We've not come at the right time, but then there's nothing on the other side we want to get to. It's an odd little place, the ferry a throwback to another time, keeping rights of way open despite ground-breaking change. We walk up to Thelwall village afterwards. An inscription on the pub records 923, when 'Edward the Elder founded a city here and called it Thelwall.' A city with a handful of residents, a ferry across the Ship Canal for 11p. We've fallen from the viaduct into an alternate world.

FOUR: ESTUARY

I'm crossing the Mersey by train at Runcorn and look out of the window to see two channels exiting towards the sea. One is wide, the spreading silver estuary of a river reaching the sea. The other seems small from above, a constrained cut of water too small for a ship. There's only a narrow spit of land between the two. Just below Irlam Locks, the Ship Canal appropriates the Mersey, taking her water and her route, much as it earlier co-opted the Irwell. The Irwell remains a landlocked river, though, whereas the Mersey breaks out again, coming to the sea under her own steam. It's a quick glimpse, this sighting of the end of the port, but it makes me think about human effort facing off against nature, about one city taking the name for a waterway, the swagger (or hubris) of calling a port yours when it borrows so much from other places. But Manchester is, I think, why the canal is there. Manchester's vision, industry driving creation. The river is there first, bringing the town. Then come other lines of commerce: road, canal, tram, train, motorway. They track each other, following the same lines of desire, to reach their destination. One takes another's resources, then a third wipes out the trading power of both of them. They will come and they will go. We will see them, or we won't. They will continue to shape our world regardless.

Sarah Jasmon

High/Low

The autumn that spiders were discovered in the porridge oats
and hard set words arrived in the post from companies **High 03:43 (5.47m)**
that had commodified themselves into existence and James out of it
– that autumn – I do not think I slept a **Low 09:46 (2.85m)** whole night through.

From a room in a tall house on a sea front – from which I did not sleep –
High 15:51 (5.68m) I see what the map told me is true: here I am only
surrounded by half as many places. Water isn't **Low 22:27 (2.35m)** 'places.'
Water lacks colonising suffixes telling Norse, telling Saxon. Telling.

In exchange: port. In exchange for half of my surrounding **High 04:45 (5.80m)**
places: The possibility of anything. Water isn't places but eats them sometimes,
takes their names like marriage: Dogger, with favours **Low 10:45 (2.46m)** of
moor peat embedded with Mesolithic barbed points.

In/out: Pebbles, seashells, Garfield phones, lost rubber ducks thrilling students of
High 16:54 (6.04m) ocean current, all those islanders with identical front doors. Water
overcoming water laid sand, reclaiming table salt from chips. Table **Low 23:15 (1.94m)**
is not the origin of salt. I look out to Dogger, past the port which took in all those

dissolute **High 05:31 (6.12m)** youths who died insane/ ladybirds the
summer before. Too much of anything tilts a plague: ladybirds, payment
demands, electricity discharged **Low 11:29 (2.07m)** by Thomas A Swift's Electric
Rifle. I meet more people, bring their names into my telephone from my

central point **High 17:27 (6.36m)** on the hard line of the semicircle. Port.

Fee Griffin

A Transition Zone

There's a picture in the family album, my aunt, full in the frame, mouth wide open, screaming, mid-laugh. There's a guy behind her feeling her arse. It's the 1970s, or early 1980s. My aunt is at work, the bloke is a colleague. They are working in manufacturing, in central London. She walked out of school into full employment at a local company. For so many reasons, good and bad, this kind of photo wouldn't be taken now.

The company was Royle's printers on Wenlock Road, London N1. I had two aunts that worked there. The building overlooked our flats.

Throughout the entire time I lived there that road was lined with factories, depots and warehouses. Building after building, with industrial, corrugated iron shutters, barred windows and big, heavy, forbidding doors. So many people who lived in our flats were employed by these places in some way at some point. Royle's stood out. One, because it was the biggest. Two, because it was fairly elegant; the entrance was rather grand as I recall. And three, it was the last building you could access from Wenlock Road. Beyond that point it was gated, heading out towards the water. All the factories on that side of the road backed out onto water. It was like we lived on an island.

It wasn't an island. It was a basin. We backed onto the Regent's Canal. Built in the 19th century, go one way and you end up in Paddington on the Grand Union route, go the other and you end up in Limehouse Docks and the Thames. These industrial spaces were originally put there because of the canal. When the rivers and canals were the arteries of industrial Britain and the ports were its beating heart.

I lived here until the mid-1990s. I never knew whether to say I was from Hackney or Islington. It didn't feel like either. Those flats felt like an island. An indeterminate space. Our dwellings were U-shaped; factories overlooking the canal flanked A and B block, old, scruffy gardens of terraced houses that posh people lived in faced C block. Our homes looked out into a big green park. Separating us from everyone – a threshold to be crossed into the outside world. By the time I left, I fucking hated that park. In the last ten years I was there it was a collision course. Avoiding my peers who'd take the piss out of me, and the mums I'd known my whole life asking questions about my fashion, education and life choices. I was a somewhat precocious, or should that be pretentious, teenager. I miss it now, I think.

The canal was another matter. It was my retreat. It was enclosed by a big abandoned industrial building and Royle's. On a weekday you would nearly always see someone smoking on the Printer's fire escape. Round the corner from Royle's you'd also glimpse the life behind those shut-off buildings that lined our street; car doors slamming, vans being loaded, people laughing and shouting, all floating on this island space.

I liked the water, the house boats, ducks and swans – they weren't of my world. I knew where everything on solid ground would take me – tangible places I could walk to or take a bus or tube. With the canal I didn't, it was like an alternative, parallel landscape with traces of a working, industrial past, but with added nature (the nearest I got to nature at that time, anyway).

An artificial gateway to the river and the sea, made for commercial purposes, the canal is by its nature a commodity. After all, they have been constructed purely for human endeavours. While we may no longer use these channels for industry, a picturesque waterway can be made into a highly prized selling point in 21st-century London. Constructed nature in the heart of the city.

There are still some companies on Wenlock Road. But now most of road is now lined with 'luxury' apartments, many boasting waterside views. The Royle Building was itself converted into flats some time ago. A quick look online and you'll find a two-bedroom apartment in the complex for around £1,000,000. The high ceilings that accommodated large, heavy printing and type-setting machines are very desirable. The bare brick walls, concrete ceilings and steel framed windows that bounced and amplified my aunts' and their workmates' laughter off the walls are authentic, industrial design features. The building is described by estate agents as iconic, which I suppose it is. And, according to one property description, "The benefit of the canal affords you scenic walking or cycling access to Angel, Broadway Market and London Fields or Victoria Park in a number of minutes whilst Shoreditch and Hoxton Square is a short walk away through the basin."

Where the Royle Building has led, others have followed. Warehouses, depots and factories have been demolished and new apartment blocks have been erected in their place along the road. The road I used to walk down is unrecognisable from my childhood or my teenage years. But there's a very stark separation in the area. My old flats, Windsor House, are half the price of a Royle's riverside abode. Some Windsor House flats still have tenants but many are now privately owned. A three-bedroom flat is priced at £500k and private rent is £2k a month, so I'm not sure how affordable this 'half price' option is.

It feels somewhat fitting that my current home, out in north Essex, is on the site of an old port, in Wivenhoe. The entrance to our 'estate' was the gateway to the port. Our garden contains the broken up rubble from the original industrial site. I too have fallen for the allure of waterside living and my money earned in London is probably pricing out someone who grew up in my new home town.

Most of the time my life now seems very, very far away from the Wenlock Basin. But on working on a series of illustrations for this book, it took me back there and compelled me to think about the constructed, commercial waterways I grew up with.

Ports for me aren't just places of arrivals and departures, they are spaces of transformation. Both immediate and slow and steady. Even if they remain working, new technology changes the bones of a port. The people and goods that ports receive and export, change according to market forces and the politics of the age. Like my childhood island and my adult home, these places are palimpsests. Built over and transformed to accommodate every new use. Layers of new construction, stories, dreams, histories coming together, shifting, mutating over time.

Ella Johnston

Before the Oil

Huddled in navy duffel coats,
we follow the Geography teacher
along the quay, past the stinking crates
of cod and plaice. Fishing boats churn
and slap the grimy harbour water.
Seagulls scream as men in yellow oilskins
shout out, *Watch your backs*, heave the catch
ashore. Wholesalers argue over bulk prices.

We are not happy with Mr. Fraser's
choice of field trip, turn away to chew
our gum and blow pink bubbles. He vetoed
our vote for a day's ski-ing in Aviemore.
We hold our noses at the stench of fish
guts and oil slicks round our feet, fret
at the irrelevance of this frozen five a.m. start.
The black oil puddles stain our brown suede boots.

Ten years later, BP and Shell take on
the city: Stetsons and burger-bar
slang along Union Street, a heliport
on the hospital roof, Dyce airport expanded for jets.
Oil rigs on the North Sea's horizon signal
a two-week-on, two-week-off lifestyle
for workers. We aren't to know –
we'll be off and away before all that.

Alison Campbell

On Marine Parade a smattering of cars under a wet grey sky. The smell of fish and chips from The Contented Sole. The Whale Hotel still standing vacant, silent. At low tide a sea fisherman stands looking out with his lures, seeking pollock among the kelp, braving the chill of an easterly, knowing the wind is no real wind. Eyemouth knows real wind. It knows European windstorms, the most severe form of extratropical cyclones that race in from the continent. In October 1881, such a windstorm took the lives of 189 local fishermen on a day now known as Black Friday. Boats were capsized or wrecked on the Hurkar rocks. Houses were destroyed. The names of the fishing boats told of hope. *Wave, Pressing Home, Guiding Star, Good Intent, Onward, Transcendence, Renown, Industry, Perseverance, Invincible, Forget-Me-Not.* Or they told of loved ones. *Alice, Christina, Janet, Margaret, Mary, Catherine, Six Brothers.* All lost. A granite monument – a broken mast – stands for those who perished at sea: 'When thou passest through waters, I will be with thee.'

Mynedd Margam, Port Talbot

I am drawn from sleep by the coo of a pigeon nesting in the guttering outside my window. Scraps of images from dreams float around the room and then fade into the dense miasma, sweet with the stench of booze and hormones. My mouth is bone dry.

It's 2005. Yesterday, the Welsh rugby team won its first Grand Slam title of my life, and celebrations ran deep into the night. Now, as I rise from the comfort of oblivion, I scramble for memories of getting home, of leaving the last or second-to-last bar. The familiar sense of dread that comes with a blank in time, a period of complete nothingness, consumes me. I am only eighteen, but this has become a regular occurrence, and I am worried because there is something in the way I drink of determined self-obliteration.

I creep across the landing and hover over the banister, listening for the hushed sounds of serious conversation. I move on to the bathroom, my arms and legs shaking, and turn the shower on, letting it warm while I brush my teeth. As the water washes over my pale, tobacco-stained skin, I probe any vague clues as to who I had seen or what I had done. I write things like 'fuck it' and 'dick head' half-consciously in the condensation formed on the shower screen. It's torture doing this, trying to piece together a picture of an irretrievable past.

I consider calling one of my friends, but I can't face it yet. I notice my phone and wallet on the bedside table, which indicates at least a trace of control. I dress and head downstairs, cross the hall and pick up my car keys from the dresser. I acknowledge the precise alignment of my trainers next to the front door. My parents are out, so I drink two pints of metallic-tasting water and smoke a cigarette in the garden, before loading my coat, camera and tripod into the boot of the silver Peugeot on the drive.

*

Fifteen miles west of Bridgend, my hometown, the Port Talbot steelworks grind and churn, spewing smoke over the Bristol Channel. It's an overwhelming landscape: iconic, dominant, apocalyptic. I recall seeing it on trips to the cinemas in Swansea and Port Talbot as a child, journeys to various sports pitches in villages and towns scattered around the M4. For all intents and purposes, the site is a living organism: it shifts and breathes, consumes and produces. At night, through the car window, it's a dreamland of shadow and flame.

I have taken recently, on mornings such as this one, to removing myself from home, from the places I know so well. Learning to drive was a watershed moment: we are no longer confined to territories within trekking distance, and so our teenage explorations have spread as far and wide as petrol money will allow. When I am feeling low, which usually occurs post-binge, I head out alone and drive aimlessly until I find somewhere to park, wallow and walk. Since starting at the sixth form college in Cardiff, where I study photography and literature, I take pictures too.

I fumble through my CDs, all new releases: Bright Eyes, Ani DiFranco, Idlewild. Jesus. Instead, I opt for the radio and likely hear of more dead troops, Tony Blair's re-election for a third term and, of course, the Welsh victory. Prince Charles is marrying Camilla next month. We've heard nothing yet of bird flu, the London bombings or Hurricane Katrina. There's a segment about a flight sergeant from Wales shot down with nine others over the desert north of

Baghdad. It's one of the worst tragedies to hit the RAF in modern times – but honestly, what did we expect?

I want to find a vantage from which to photograph the steelworks, but first I follow the dual carriageway around the outskirts of town, then cut through the centre, intending to retrace my steps and kick my memory into gear. I survey the drab exterior of the last club I recall entering and remember barking at a man I thought was the spit of Shane Williams. I see some sticky concoction spilled down the front of a girl at the bar, and the look of disgust on a friend's face as I garble together some shit joke about his sister. There are daffodils trampled black on the concrete where we'd queued.

I pass an army recruitment poster on my left and the Co-op Bank on my right. I resolve to check my statement. I light a cigarette and slow down outside the kebab shop – was I banging on the glass? I catch an image of myself running along the pavement, crossing the road and skidding into the wall by Spar. Two passers-by shaking their heads. I touch my hip and unleash a wave of pain through my side. How did I not notice this wound? The lights turn green and I put my foot down, leaving behind these brief and humiliating illuminations. I race towards the motorway.

*

The steelworks appear on the coast like a huge industrial theme park. Grey and charcoal tubes curving into the ether, lattice towers and tracks like water slides plummeting from tall platforms to the ground. All this obscured by a silver mist, a poisonous vapour floating over the rooftops of Port Talbot, which unfold like a faded patchwork quilt beyond the elevated guardrail. I take a pen from the glove compartment and write 'theme park' on the back of my hand, a flicker of something rising from childhood. Someone on the radio is talking about *Doctor Who* – a series is returning to our screens for the first time since 1989.

Once I've past the town – which spills away from the docks built on the south-east side of the River Afan in the 1830s – I exit the M4, U-turn at the roundabout and join the lines of traffic flowing in the opposite direction. In a few minutes, I turn off again and head blindly for Margam Mountain, the crest of which, I think, must afford perfect views of the landscape below. I don't actually know the name of the mountain, nor do I have any idea of where to park or walk in order to reach the summit, but there is something hopeful in this: boundaries vanish when you know nothing of the labels of a place.

I drive along roads I've never seen before. Soon, I spot signs for a riding school and Margam Stones Museum, home to a collection of Celtic crosses dug up from the surrounding pasture. The most famous of these is the Cross of Conbelin, which dates from around AD 1000 and displays plaitwork patterns and a vision of hunting: ancient memories cut into rock. It's strange to think of wild communities wandering in the darkness of a long-dead forest, making records of their lives.

I wind down the window and light another cigarette. I'm fighting back a wave of nausea, listening now to the uplifting anarchy of a Californian punk band, when a young man walks out of the trees to the right. He's wearing a grey hooded top, discoloured by soil, and is carrying a plastic bag filled with something heavy: cans of lager, perhaps – or maybe not. Smoke from his rollie, which is hanging from the corner of his mouth, billows around the peak of his cap. He walks 20 yards or so along the ridge of a shallow ditch, before crossing the road and climbing over a gate into an adjacent field.

There's a distinctive rhythm to his long, lolloping strides, a spring in his step that does nothing to alter the impression of sadness made by his appearance on this deserted country lane. As I write now, I picture a young man from Bridgend – the suicide capital of Britain, according to the press – sitting on a step outside his parents' kitchen. He finishes a cup of coffee in the early-morning sun, stubs out his cigarette and swings a rucksack over his shoulder. On the drive, in front of the house, he takes one last look at home and then walks away, into the woods backing onto a large industrial estate.

*

I pull over into a layby. I've covered at least part of the lower region of the mountain and decide to continue on foot from here. I take my equipment from the boot, load a canister of black and white film in the back of the camera and leave my jacket where it is. My hands are still trembling. Beads of sweat form immediately on my forehead when my thoughts return to the previous night. I lock the car and think involuntarily, as I often do, of putting a gun in my mouth and pulling the trigger.

I walk a little while, then join a footpath and begin to climb. Before long, I arrive at an open plateau, upon which are the impressive ruins of an old chapel. Capel Mair, as it's known, was built by local monks in a style indicative of the 14th century, but it's thought another church may have preceded it. In the Middle Ages, pilgrims travelled from faraway to pay homage to a famous statue of the Virgin Mary; after the Reformation, Catholics used the site to worship in secret. Bodies have been found nearby.

The weather is overcast, but the physical excursion keeps the cold at bay. My heart is thumping and I'm beginning to think I might actually throw up. I hear voices rising over the walls. I move quickly to re-join the track, which looks to wind further up the mountain, but as I skip round I stumble on a slab of flat rock and crunch over the debris beneath my feet. There's a commotion in the chapel. Two men appear and walk towards me. One is wearing a long black coat, with his hair tied back in a ponytail; the other is bald, his military jacket torn and shabby.

Fuckin' hell, boy, you gave us a fright.
What you creepin' for, lad? Nothin' to fear by yer. Just a

couple of old fuckers smokin' a J.

Lovely mornin', innit?

I explain I want to photograph the steelworks and ask if they know the quickest route to the top of the mountain.

What you wanna photograph that shithole for? Take a picture of us, mun.

They stretch their arms around one another's shoulders and smile, revealing rows of crooked brown teeth. I raise my camera obediently and snap three shots – click, click, click.

Straight up there and carry on over, butt. Nice camera that.

Watch out for the dead monks, right – you'll know them by their cloaks. Grumpy fuckers, they are.

Take care, boyo.

*

I'm surrounded by trees. There's no sign of the path, and the slope, which I'm roughly half-way up, is very steep. I'm almost on all fours. Behind me, at the bottom of the incline, is a broken wall covered in moss and lichen. There's a telephone pole, too, upon which a crow has just alighted. I stop to rest, retching twice into a pile of mulched leaves, and watch a hare dart diagonally towards the top of the hill. A mist falls over my eyes and the environment tilts askew. The taste of sick helps me retrieve another shred of memory: I'm vomiting next to a car parked outside the club. The bouncer pushes me back from the door and tells me to go home.

I emerge from the woods and walk the final stretch to the summit with relief and anticipation. I suddenly recall a childhood visit to Margam Park, which can't be far from here. The nightmarish miniature dwellings of the Fairytale Village, where me and my brother played. I got lost in the maze and was found by three women speaking only in Welsh – I was crying and couldn't understand a word. When they handed me over to my father, he splayed his fingers and smacked the backs of my bare legs. There's Margam Castle, too, formerly owned by the Talbot family, who built the docks that defined the town.

It's a pleasing coincidence that this family, which gave its name to the communities amalgamated along the coast, was directly related to Henry Fox Talbot, a photography pioneer who contributed to both the scientific and artistic development of the medium. When I point my lens at a place, selecting which features to include in the frame in order to best tell the story I want to convey, I feel connected to that landscape. I am taking from it and giving it something in return. It doesn't matter if it's the first time I've visited the location – relationships can form in an instant, just as they are honed over a lifetime. Photographing an area that shares its name with a person who helped make this experience possible feels somehow significant.

At the edge of the mountain, looking out over the Bristol Channel, the conurbation is as breathtaking in its way as I'd imagined. I see symmetrical rows of silver and beige industrial units, massive hanger-like structures and plots of derelict land. There are cars of various colours, people going about their business. I see a rugby pitch, a social club, and off to the west, beyond the smoke and flame, the town itself. The waters are calm and pale. Somewhere, I've heard, is a cursed wall, the only remains of a Medieval farmhouse, which if collapsed would take the entire town tumbling with it.

Just down from my current location is a radar site, erected as part of the defensive strategy during World War II. I fix my camera to the tripod, which I've borrowed from my photography teacher, and scan the landscape through the viewfinder. Playing with the depth of field on my prime lens, I feel something like a radar station, an aerial picking up stories and messages, patterns and connections, from the world below. I pause to light another cigarette and start capturing images.

The Welsh writer Christopher Meredith, in his debut novel *Shifts* (1988), which is set amid a declining steel community, describes an almost supernatural occurrence. His central character, Keith, a local history enthusiast, spends an afternoon wandering the length of his hometown with some blank paper and a pen in his pocket. He registers the divisions between old and new, and racks his brain for dates and previous formations of the streets around him. He removes his glasses so the picture blurs, which allows him to travel through time, editing and reimagining the physical environment as he goes. It's like MR James.

I distort the focus on the lens and swivel round in order to absorb the full panorama. Facing the valley behind me, I see cairns and hillforts, people sharing meat and twisting metal into intricate shapes. They're burying their dead. As I pull the camera west, I see barrows and defensive strongholds, mountain pasture and livestock. This land is marked by the history of Christianity, materials drawn from the earth and stacked for worship. I see monks mining coal.

As the camera settles on the coastal plain, I see the natural harbour, the river estuary, where coal and sheep are shipped through South Wales, to Bristol and the West Country. I see tramlines like scars and the emerging hustle and bustle. I see the first incarnation of the steelworks and the nearby colliery, where 87 men were killed in a gas explosion at the end of 19th century – 15 bodies remain beneath towers that stand now like monuments. I see the diversion of the river, sand dunes levelled and marshland drained, the shifting skyline, people protesting on the streets. I see ships the size of factories turned towards the open sea.

Over the next ten minutes, I shoot an entire reel of film.

*

I sit down on the damp grass and smoke yet another cigarette. I think of the people I know who work at the steelworks. Meredith's title, *Shifts*, is a reference to monotonous routines and his characters' lack of control. Factory work has been used as a threat at numerous points in my life: *pull yourself together*, or else. I, however, see honour and pride in it, camaraderie and community, but it's not what I want.

Since starting at the sixth form college – an expensive and unfair last chance, paid for with steel money – I have discovered a real passion for art and literature, and my priorities have changed; this, I think, has set me adrift from many of my friends. These days, I so often struggle for common ground and conversation, which might be part of why I drink with such recklessness: to loosen up and stay connected. On mornings like this one, though, I want nothing more than to move on and obliterate my past. No friends, no family, no history, no shame.

If my camera could show me the future of this place, I would see more upheaval: thousands of jobs at risk, Labour politicians on the picket line, a vote out of Europe. I would see a world-famous artist moving through the streets at night, spraying a stark image of climate change on the side of a garage: a child dancing amid swirls of falling ash; crowds gathered for months, scrambling for selfies. I would see myself on the mountain, taking photos and shooting time-lapse videos of smoke erupting into the sky, as if from a volcano. I would see that I'll never develop the film that I shot today, but that's beside the point.

Tim Cooke

Irvine Harbour

Finer years have weathered your jetties
before that footbridge's purposeful arc
lost heart. A sabotaged path,
blown apart from dynamite land
shrivels, scared of its factory past.

Under ripped planks, around tired posts
water sleeves everything. Currents, unmarked
unravel bare islets, rub wharves, leave banks.
This thuggish Clyde slugs in
two feeder rivers, and can out-stare
forever and Ireland.

Not trusting this firth, I pocket slow time.
Who'd sail or swim here
without plotting a course?
You trace me your day, your week
bouy up your year. Waters rise. With nothing
to channel or navigate, I worry the way
you might chart my escape.

Beth McDonough

A Creative Climate

Art doesn't just have to reside in the capitals. Like Florence, Chicago and Barcelona, Bristol has established itself a world art destination. Where you go to Florence for the frescoes, Chicago for Anish Kapoor's *Cloud Gate* and Barcelona for the Gaudí, you visit Bristol for the street art.

Bristol's history as a port has given the city an internationalist outlook. It was England's second biggest city by the 18th century and, by the 21st, has a reputation as one of the most vibrant and cosmopolitan places in Britain.

History marks Bristol as a vital maritime port. Ships left Bristol to found colonies in the 'new world'. Merchants made vast fortunes in the trade of sugar cane, rum, tobacco and cocoa, though let's not forget, all of which were products of the trade in slaves.

But the city has a history of challenging the status quo. As a centre of the early Methodist movement, Bristol's New Room, originally built in 1739, is the oldest Methodist Chapel in the world. This location was used by founding father John Wesley as a place to meet, preach and to speak out against the slave trade.

Bristol is synonymous for individuality and innovation. By the 19th century, Isembard Kingdom Brunel made his mark on the ever-expanding city with grand designs that still inspire. In the 20th century, Concorde was built, as are Rolls-Royce cars still, and now the city boasts a contemporary cutting-edge arts scene that welcomes artists from around the world.

Artist and illustrator SPZero76 says the community around the city gives Bristol an overall creative vibe. "Bristol, like Brighton and parts of London, is very open minded and liberal. I think this allows culture and alternative lifestyles to thrive," he says.

While you have the iconic harbourside and Brunel -designed Clifton suspension bridge, which spans the

River Avon to the west of the city centre, the joy in this place lies with the way old and new ideas can sit side by side. SPZero76 cites the architecture and free spaces found in the city as an additional factor in his creative journey. "There are plenty of spaces to practice spray painting in Bristol. Without these areas I wouldn't have been able to hone my skills and learn."

Bristol's reputation as an art city has been firmly established over recent years with some modern-day key players. One of these is Stephen Hayles, director of Upfest gallery and festival.

The artistic, outward-looking atmosphere of the city inspired Hayles and friends to launch Upfest. The free art festival has been showcasing global artists on the street art scene since 2008. It initially started small, with 40-plus artists taking over Bristol venue the Tobacco Factory, for a day. The following year it expanded into more Bristol venues and on to the city's streets. Originally conceived as an urban paint festival, the once modest 'painting day' turned into a 48-hour show with indoor and outdoor music stages and 'live' urban and contemporary art demos. It has grown into an international art event with 400 artists, from more than 70 countries, live painting over two days, across around 60,000 square feet of the city with 50,000 visitors.

"The community has, on the whole, been very supportive of Upfest," Hayles states. "We're lucky in that as a port city Bristol has a diverse population and therefore a wide and varied range of influences. There are lots of cities around the country who are now doing street art festivals but I believe we'll always have that history. And because of that artists want to come here."

SPZero76 agrees. "I moved to Bristol in 1996 to do a BA in illustration at the University of the West of England. Bristol has a massive art scene. It's notorious. I talked to artists in Paris a few years ago and they said they watched the Bristol scene more than the London scene."

"As a city Bristol is a creative, progressive place," Hayles continues. "Some of that vibe originates in the underground music scene with the likes of Massive Attack and Roni Size etc. The music went hand in hand with graffiti and street art. Then there's that artist who we don't like to talk about…" he jokes.

The artist Hayles is referring to is Banksy. And while Hayles is keen to point out "we really wouldn't be doing what we're doing now if it wasn't for Banksy leading the way", the Upfest director is mindful that Bristol's art scene is more than one artist.

"Banksy has done great things to promote this style of art and the contemporary cultural reputation of Bristol. People often ask me if I'd like him to come to Upfest. In the early days I'd have been delighted, but then I think 'what would the headline be?' What about the hundreds of other artists taking part? Mind you, what a great problem to have."

After celebrating ten years of the festival, Hayles and the Upfest team have decided to refresh the event. From

2020 artists will no longer be taking over the city for the weekend, rather the festival will run over three weeks.

"Upfest weekend has got so busy. So much so that the council were looking at shutting streets down over the two days. We don't want to disrupt the city, so we've decided to spread it out. We've rejigged the format so you can watch a lot of the buildings being done by the artists over a longer period," says Hayles.

The success of Upfest led Hayles to open the Upfest gallery to celebrate the work of festival artists all year round. "Entry criteria is very simple. To appear in the gallery you have had to have painted at the festival. The gallery has been a go-to destination for art tourists."

"Art tourism is huge in Bristol," Hayles observes. "I don't have the stats but my estimate is at least a third of tourists coming to the city are coming for the art."

So, where does the art pilgrim go to in Bristol? "You need to visit two places," says Hayles. "Go to Stokes Croft which has the more traditional graffiti. Then come south of the river to Bedminster and check out more curated street art pieces."

While Bristol is a city with a rich heritage, boasting iconic buildings, historic boats and trade roots, Hayles believes that it's most definitely the contemporary street art that makes the city unique and is attracting the modern day tourist to Bristol.

"The great thing about street art is one person can make one statement that a million people agree with," says Hayles.

"The difference between street art and a museum is people have to make a choice to go into a building. And there are people who don't like those environments. If something is on the street, you are directly confronted by it. It sparks a conversation, it's more engaging on a direct level."

Just Below Mousehole

The sea offers up
out of its grey lapping

a school
of yellow kayaks

a flock
of buoyant people

paddling
into startled view

round the lonely
rocky outcrop

where we crouch—
about to offer up

your ashes to the sea.
How you would have laughed.

Janet Hatherley

Journey to a Wivenhoe Resonance

Images of the port of embarkation and the first arrival in England are milestones as we head 'Home' to attend a Preparatory School at Felixstowe that is to be life for the next few years.

The Bombay dockside is busy with a jostling crowd. The outgoing Viceroy with his plumed helmet, shining black and gold encrusted ceremonial dress and the long sword at his belt, climbs aboard the SS *Strathmore* to the military band's rendition of 'God Save the King'. Memsahib and Ayah cling to each other and weep on the quay before they part, and my mother walks up the gangplank to join us. Even as the ship disappears into the haze, the long years of the Raj are coming to an end, and Herr Hitler, in 1936, is building a brutal new Empire in Europe.

On this journey, the rusty steel of the ship cuts through the Indian Ocean, and as many as a dozen porpoises race in and out of the bow waves. On through the Suez Canal to the Mediterranean, where one dark night, we sight Stromboli, the volcanic island, hurling red-hot lava from the crater to light the sulphurous clouds, penetrating the atmosphere of the mind.

Finally, our ship eases gently to the dockside at Tilbury, still a thriving shipping port, on the mighty Thames, two trusty tugs pulling, pushing at her rusty skirts. Warps are flung ashore; a gangplank spans the oily gap, and we walk onto solid ground, a muddied dockside in the rain.

Nearby, a steam train awaits, panting on the rusty rails. Luggage has been stowed in the guard's van, the press of goodbyes has eased and the last peeling, painted wooden door has slammed. The guard waves his red flag. His whistle shrills. The wheels slip chu-chu-chu on the shiny rails and steam hisses from the thrusting pistons. Heads crane out of windows lowered by worn leather straps, gouts of smoke billow back above us as we gathering speed towards Saint Felix, the prep school in our next port of call, Felixstowe.

In 1938 it is a short walk from school to the Felixstowe Docks on the River Orwell. There is no hint of today's container port, but a string of aircraft hangars, sheds and slipways host a growing base for Flying Boats. The clumsy monsters splash heavily into the choppy seas, and anchor near the shoreline. Pale ladies in white, flouncy dresses and men in suits donning their jackets in the chilly breeze, try to keep their balance as they are ferried ashore in rowing boats to reception at this early airport.

*

The estuary tides flow in and out; a regular heartbeat in a changing world. Through the winter daylight hours, the summer solstice, Antarctic ice and jet streams, the river runs constant to the sea. It was not always so. The river has seen the tip of ice ages, and East Anglia once joined the coast of Germany.

DAY ONE

It is 2018. This January morning it is eight o'clock, and daylight reluctantly suggests that curtains should be drawn. Fog obliterates the world. No one can see the other bank 200 yards away. What would our ancestors think of this – the earth, the sun, and the sky hidden on purpose by a grumpy God waking with an aching head?

The river does not care as daylight strengthens and the mist begins to thin. A gull flies by and disappears. A darker shade of grey resolves into a muddy bank and as the tide drifts in the old fishing boat begins to float; a reminder of earlier days when the river was buzzing with livelihoods and trade. The water and the tide recall the smacks, full of sprats, decks awash, chasing each other up to Colchester docks in November and folks from Wivenhoe walking to Brightlingsea to track across the mud collecting oysters for a humble meal.

They have seen the barges carrying cargoes of straw or bricks and will recall them sailing up the creek to Ballast Quay until the railways took over, and the tidal stream silted up. A small coal yard took over and became, in turn, a yellow-flowered muddy stream at the centre of a small collection of houses.

Small coasters, too, smoke and steam blown by the wind, crept up on the tide to disgorge evil-smelling dust clouds of fertiliser at Rowhedge. Others went on to the Hythe at Colchester carrying bricks from Belgium and timber from Russia. Through a bedroom window at night, these little ships, all lit up, seemed like ocean liners. The crews would wave as they passed and call greetings in strange languages.

"Nazdrovia," (Welcome – pleased to meet you) shouted from a coaster carrying timber at the height of the cold war; the Russians were real people after all.

There are many other winter high points for the river – the arrival of Santa Claus on a Dutch Tjalk; the gift of a lone seal and the wedge of geese migrating to the Baltic from their near-by winter feeding grounds.

The sun is flying low to the west, and the streaky clouds display all those colours; the pinks, the dark blues and the oranges of our beloved sunsets, dressing the fiery orb, now dipped behind the trees for another long, long night. The tide breathes in and out quietening our frantic heads, and the river sleeps.

DAY TWO

A bright and frosty morning; the tide is low, and the surface mirrors the sharply etched reflection of the fishing boat well aground on the far side. The empty buoys spread out downstream wait for a purpose in their lives. The rising sun illuminates the jetties and their rails reaching out into the water. There is still a misty cloak on the trees, and the church tower in Fingringhoe shimmers in the growing sunlight.

A day for contemplation or ritual; for walking the dog and a chat with other owners while Molly and Rufus sniff and take stock.

"Nice to see Molly, well wrapped up. Is she better?"

"Fine now thanks. The vet's bill was a bit of a shock, but you're worth it aren't you Molly, love?"

The quiet returns until a train hoots as it approaches the unmarked crossing at the village edge and slowly the world comes to life. Commuters trudge greyly to their trains and purgatory (computer screens or stuffy boardroom meetings, their life) returning home later – the day gone – roads taken and the children already in bed, unaware of the kiss goodnight.

As the mist clears, the breeze picks up, ruffling the incoming tide with a sprinkle of stardust. In the summer this could be any Regatta day over the last 100 years with a mix of sailing craft racing for fun and brownie points. 'One' designs from Brightlingsea and Wivenhoe in the 1930s, the Thames barges, the old gaffers and the fishing smacks keeping their traditions alive, with modern yachts and sailing dinghies heading the future.

Regattas remain one of the bright spots of the river calendar. The crowds come for the fun of the fair; the pints of ale and the chance of catching up.

"Nice to see you, dear. How's your mother?"

"Well enough thanks; still a bit of a tartar – can't do anything for herself when I'm around – perfectly capable the rest of the time."

Then there is the brass band on the quay – all polish and Oompa, Oompa.

The raft and rowing races survive but the greasy pole, the tug of war across the river; the Black Buoy warriors against those stalwarts from the Whalebone at Fingringhoe and the round-the-village pram race, once traditional fare, have succumbed to 'elf and safety – God 'elp us.

Now it is the gigs, four oarsmen and a coxswain sponsored by villages along the estuary, racing for fitness and for glory and a flood of kayaks and canoes replacing the rockers on their jet skis who used to roar up from Brightlingsea on sleepy Sunday afternoons.

Three boys in dirty shorts mudslide and splash into the water on the other bank with shouts of pretended fear, and of glee. One poor swimmer only just manages to swim back and climb exhausted to a pontoon this side. Summer thoughts.

And on this winter's day, the sun has already gone. In the darkened sky, the half-moon peers through wispy clouds and the few stars strong enough to penetrate the sulphurous glow of street lights flicker in the haze. The river stays calm. The tide has come and gone and begins to rise again. Quiet, immutable, reflecting inwardly.

DAY THREE

The wind shrieks through the rigging of the mud-berthed yachts and the clatter of loose halyards add a stuttered racket to the waves chasing across the river; wind against tide.

Headed into the gale young Mrs J with her two girls, warmly clad, march past on the dot towards Millfields School along the river and up the hill half a mile away.

"Come along Jess. Don't want to keep Mrs Thompson waiting, do we?"

On days like this many a fisherman has been lost at sea and many a mother or wife left grieving; many a child left fatherless. There have been many tragedies off our shores; the loss of the fishing fleets from Barking to Brightlingsea, (marked by the plaques in All Saints Church there,) in 1863, when 60 fishermen perished in violent storms off the Dutch coast. The sea takes few prisoners, and as recently as December 1982 a ferry and a cargo ship collided off Harwich; six lives lost.

Ships have been driven ashore with the fledgeling coastguards attempting rescues from the raging seas. Others have chosen to "rescue" casks of brandy, carried through the mythical tunnels to the Black Buoy or The Rose and Crown or the cargo of Bechstein grand pianos, floated ashore still smelling of French polish and pride.

Yesterday a strong-willed sailor took his "Barrow-boat" into the gusts to publicise his new venture with a memorable photo shoot.

Today a contemporary young woman launches her Kayak taking her fight to the elements before stowing it and jogging home, sweating for a shower and a spray of L'Oréal.

The river and the tides of Wivenhoe will remember, too, the Victorian steam yachts lining the banks; mud-berthed for the winter, including *Rosabelle*, *Invicta*, *Venetia*, and many more – such grand names. Did Arthur Sullivan and his friend Gilbert from their house in Brightlingsea visit those floating palaces on occasion and entertain the elegant soirées with jokey verse and classic piano pieces, perhaps even on one of those 'rescued' grands?

Into the 20th century, when 'J' Class yachts wintered here. At least two, owned by Sir Thomas Lipton were named *Shamrock*. They were designed to challenge for the |America's Cup, before and after WW1. Many a local fisherman sailed as crew in the races, and chose the famous names for their own fishing boats, including mine in the early 1970s, and now awaiting a rebuild at Harker's Yard in Brightlingsea.

So, raise a glass to old boats, and a quiet evening. Forget the blue flicker of TV screens through netted curtains and the inevitable posturing of celebrities.

The tide retreats and the wind slowly dies. A glimmer of weak sunlight paints a golden moon-face on the wave-ploughed mud. A skein of geese arrows across the sky, still black from the retreating storm but promising a brighter day on the morrow. The tides will ebb and flow. The river will be there.

Bryan Thomas

Marinetraffic.com

On the horizon, you see vessels pass left to right, rounding
Land's End along the north-bound shipping lane, two miles wide.

Containers heading for Dublin, Liverpool, Swansea are tracked online.
They mustn't deviate from the lane into the two-mile no-go area,

like a central reservation, where fishing fleets (orange symbols)
from Newlyn, Brixham, Roscoff make free; then a two mile wide

south-bound shipping lane but eyes can't see that far.
On the screen, lines of colour-coded ships move along

their designated seaways: Iceland's a cluster of orange boats
fishing for cod at minus 6. A stream of ships flows along the Channel

in both directions: a tanker called Phoenix is sailing from St Petersburg
to Istanbul, another from Antwerp to Gibraltar.

Blue circles denote ships hove-to along the coast, waiting out there
for work. Many more in the Arabian Gulf sit it out

till the price of oil rises or falls. Across the Atlantic,
a yacht race (purple symbols) and convoys carrying cargoes.

Invisible traffic.
        No symbol for whales.

Rebecca Gethin

An empty road. A single track. A fishing store. No vehicles beyond this point. A crooked line of telegraph poles links the dry stone walls of cattle pasture with the higher grounds to the west and south. The small harbour faces east across Sandside Bay, past the village of Reay. Reay from the Gaelic 'Reidh', a flat place, or 'Ratha', a fort or enclosure, or from the Norse 'Ra', a boundary marker, or 'Vra', a nook or corner. Or perhaps 'Ra', an old word for the yardarm of a boat. The fishing industry and north-coast trading route connected Fresgoe with Orkney, Shetland, Iceland, Norway and beyond. And across the water, the domed modernism of the Dounreay nuclear facility where uranium and plutonium are still held on site. Known as 'exotics', this cargo requires a security presence, and is transported by rail to Sellafield, Cumbria, for reprocessing. Irradiated nuclear fuel particles have been found on the seabed near the plant. Particles wash ashore. Local beaches are accessible to the public. Officially, some are listed as 'closed'.

Southampton

Ignored, in a corner between the road and the working area for rail freight stand the vacant skeletons of last year's cow parsley, ragwort, and fat hen. Grey from roadside dust and bleached by the sun they are propped up by gorse and bramble. Buddleia and blackthorn are enmeshed further back towards the roadway fence, with the edges of the impenetrable network of flora and plastic litter lined by a concrete walkway on all sides. Above it looms the reason this site of exclosure can exist. The area is not completely fenced off but left to flourish in filthy exuberance precisely because the matte grey legs of the pylon prevent any further development here.

Powerlines trail off to the horizons in the north and west.

"The starlings love that one. Always chattering up there before going to roost by the causeway." Mick tosses an empty spill kit bag into the back of the van and steps closer to peruse the shrubs.

"There's three or four kinds of mosses here," he says, bending at the waist to get a closer look. "I've seen common toadflax and groundsel over there as well."

Around the base of the metal security fence is a bank of detritus blown across from the road. Cars and articulated trucks barrel past nosily as we take in the contents of this poor man's verge, the grey desaturated soil pitched steeply on both sides. The remnants of other wildflowers poke through, fighting the suffocation of dust, grit and anything else kicked up off the potholed tarmac. The scars where ivy has been recently ripped from the fence mark its uprights in both directions. An attempt at diligent tidiness in the workplace.

"There's none at the moment, but you get a lot of poppies along here. The turbulent air from the lorries is perfect for seed dispersal. They don't need birds or mammals to spread them, our transport system does it all year round."

Lucky, I suppose. The only wild mammal I've seen here is a fox.

We spend a while pointing out different species of plant in the chaotic palimpsest of branches, tendrils and leaves in various stages of decay. Amongst the dogwood, hawthorn, teasels and rosehip, I see blue grape hyacinth, celandines and bluebells not yet unfurled. The edge of the path is lined with cleavers and half-mulched meadowgrass. I tread carefully on the matrix of brambles and lean in to confirm a rowan sapling that must have first come into leaf last spring. So much condensed into one spot. The space, probably 30 feet square is like a fissure in the concrete. From it, an eruption of things lain dormant spills out above ground.

A gust of wind triggers distant alarms high up on the cranes before it finds us, a mile inland. The cranes work unseen beyond the false horizon of container stacks. Only their static A-frames are visible from here.

Back to work.

The van is filthy like most vehicles in the port. Running over the cracks and potholes on land long reclaimed from the salt marsh, soil and water will find their way through. Dust from the roads is brought in by trucks and cars, and litter is picked from bins by gulls and jackdaws. I let my left arm hang, tapping the outside of the door with my fingertips. Mick shifts into reverse and turns the van. SAINTS FC is etched onto his battered yellow hard hat with permanent marker, and the oval lenses of his glasses are cataracted with fine scratches and the residue of chemical cleaning agents. Borrowed hi-viz overalls frame the annotated risk assessments on my lap. The faint diesel smell reminds me of the days of working here full-time. Of having no WIP or looming deadline, just a 60-hour working week that paid for nights out and mountainbike trips every Sunday. The bad old days. The all or nothing days.

"I found a nest of slow worms by the pond over there," Mick says, gesturing only with his line of sight, now fixed on a chaotic outcrop of buddleia and blackberry beside the new training centre.

"Where would they have come from?"

"I don't know, mate." The van surges feebly in first gear as we pass the portacabins.

I lean forward to see a little better.

"I mean, they're landlocked by tarmac."

The hidden pond is an oasis in a desert of concrete, flagstones, gravel sprayed with weedkiller, and razorwired fences. The dark green of the Freightliner cranes looms high to our right side. Half a mile of rail stock is being shunted slowly into position. As we wait at the junction to Dock Road, more straddle carriers drop boxes beyond the fence ahead. These 40-foot long containers are brought from a ship or from somewhere unseen in the endless rows of stacks that dominate the landscape here. One, two or three high, the containers encroach on any perspective.

A shadow strikes the road in front of the van and we both lean forward to look up and out through the filthy windscreen. We see a woodpigeon, wings tucked as it rides a westerly gust. It pulls skyward then drops behind the stack, lost to the cold pathways between each row and their hard shade.

The van revs higher as Mick changes down into second gear and we take the first exit at the roundabout. The stacks, on our left now, are a faded patchwork of steel and damaged paint. A lifetime of sea air and rough handling anywhere from Chicago to Shanghai. It is standardisation writ large in steel, with acronyms unknowable and unnecessary to the public lives playing out beyond the entrance to the port.

"The peregrine's been notable by its absence." Mick's eyes find the outstretched hand of the security guard as we come to a stop. We flash our photo ID passes before the bed of the van is checked for stowaways, and a mirror swiped underneath the chassis. We simultaneously slide our passes into the top pockets of our overalls and the guard waves us through the hinged gate and onto the quay.

"It could be the same one you saw over the reserve," Mick continues, eyes looking out at the flashing lights of cranes, anticipating the movements of the straddle carriers that roar beside us along these vast containership berths. The port is many things, but none more sensory than this. Activity everywhere. Seen from above, the movements of the cranes and straddle carriers and berth vehicles would make concentric logical patterns, transporting freight from ship to crane to stack to truck to train. But looking out at it, laterally, one is in it: absolutely within the kind of activity that could crush this van and us with it. Containers are lifted from the hull of the ship to the brickpaved lanes beside us. The weight of each load is so massive I can only think it as an abstract concept, and yet it swings above us on cables guided by a man in overalls the same colour as ours.

Mick doublechecks a switch on the dash. Satisfied the orange beacons are flashing on the roof, he changes into third gear and forces himself to settle back into his seat.

"The nest cam showed the peregrines did fledge the year before last, so it might be a young one that's made its own territory near the marshes rather than here. There aren't as many pigeons or blackheaded gulls as there used to be."

Mick tells me about the pigeon carcasses left around the nestbox, pointing up to the last crane on this part of the quay to indicate that it was, for a few seasons at least, the place the peregrines had made their home.

"They'd sit right up on top of the A-frame. Three hundred foot up on the new Liebherr cranes. Good views of their prey up there, that's for sure."

With seatbelts firm across our chests, it's almost impossible to comprehend the scale of the equipment outside. The only real hint at what is up there, hidden from view by the roof of the van, are the ladders leading up, and up, and up.

We stop on a promontory exposed to the wind and free from overhead activity. The Knuckle, as it's known, is a fenced area filled with unthinkably large crane components lying prostrate on trailers with soft tyres. The van is buffeted by another gust and Mick slides out to conduct his checks of the area. I wind down the window and peer out at the choppy water through the unglassed slot. This is a point of convergence, where fresh water from the River Test and Bartley Water are salined by moon fuelled tides. The surface is a dark blue grey where Southampton Water funnels between docks, military hards, and unkempt beaches before eventually becoming The Solent.

"We still get oystercatchers," says Mick, placing his gloves on the spare seat between us. "And there are always blackheaded gulls in the water on the corner here, two or three hundred of them sometimes."

Starting the engine and releasing the handbrake, Mick edges the van forward. As we approach the quay wall with no fence between us and the water, a hundred or so gulls come into view, bobbing silently against the breeze and now all turning to look up at us.

"The breeding plumage is coming in on some of them," he says, reversing then turning the van. "But if you're going to write about them, don't forget their heads aren't actually black. They're more of a chocolate brown."

We continue around the SCT5 roadway which marks the southeast boundary of the container terminal. Outside it, a shifting hierarchy of other companies mark their territory from here to the mouth of the estuary. Beyond the remit of our day's work are the cruise terminals, scrubbed clean and gleaming synthetic in the pale March sunlight. Acres of new cars wait for a ferry to somewhere else. Opposite them, across the water, are a mosaic of coastline ecologies, from blackthorn covered edgelands to a sewage works and housing estate, walled off from high tides and my gaze.

We wait for a moment as the automated security gate folds open. The van creeps forward into the holding area and we are flanked on our right side by a barrier of concrete slabs slotted between tall iron uprights. Mick calls it the Berlin Wall and explains how, behind it, the old dry dock has been repurposed for scrap metal storage. Mountains of rusted iron cast shadows over Dock Road before they are swiftly craned with a huge mechanised claw onto a vessel bound for China.

Mick looks for any last oil spills or equipment out of place. I tick some boxes, scribble on the paper and look for cormorants, kestrels and the kingfisher Mick has seen here during the summer. He stays quiet as I recount the time a buzzard was mobbed by herring gulls, the squawking mass driving the raptor down into the water from above. I scribble something else, then close the folder.

The road back to the office is quiet and we drive very slowly, watching the sun play out over the unsmooth surface of the water. A quick double toot of a horn draws our gaze to the side mirror. Another berth vehicle undertakes us at five times our speed, an open hand resting against the driver's window in thanks. It is only the second person we have needed to engage with on this job, and it strikes me that despite the size of this place, and the abundance of activity, this activity is fundamentally opposed to that in the ecosystems of its peripheries. The machinery of the port is connected through the logic of economy: of shift patterns, annual bonuses and well-serviced equipment.

The liberated spaces emerging spontaneously and unannounced in the cracks of the port suggest what kind of landscape has been renounced. In the Midlands cities of Nottingham, Leicester and Coventry, where industries have been lost to new technologies, a rebranding, or a reappropriation of the industrial landscape has occurred. These new old cities have made space for civic life and wildlife alike, connected by corridors and registered in the discourse of a new aesthetic. In Southampton, the founding principles of the city are still very much alive. Trees are rare. Hedges are replaced with miles of wire fence. And with the paralysing price of land here, how does one negotiate the dominance of concrete?

Another vast ship is brought into position by tugs, its stay here a caesura in a perpetual journey around the globe. At the quay wall, herring, blackheaded and lesser blackbacked gulls patrol the portside hull as if it were a cliff, scarred with repair work in various stages of oxidation. The wall of matte black paint is staggeringly large, not only its sheer bulk but the ten high stacks of containers improbably poised across the deck, totally eclipsing the far shoreline. The ship's contents are sealed, revealed only at their destination. To get them there, the land too must be sealed: from the brickpaved quay to the tarmacked lanes that connect this place to the evergrowing network of roadways beyond it. The port is a nodal point that favours this particular kind of system: closed, predictable, linear. Those who adhere to a different logic, those reliant on rhizomes and untidy connections are left to persist where they can: silently, with indifference, and for unknowable durations.

Mark Ranger

Margaret Smithe
Makes Her Mark

(On a ship scratched into a church pillar in Wiveton)

All the days he is away

when the water ebbs from the marshes

she comes to church to see her ship

to touch the grooves she scored there

months ago with an iron nail

as long as her ring finger

filched from the shipyard.

As her fingers press each tiny, grainy furrow,

she longs for a strong mast, for

the prow as purposeful as it was

when they set sail, the little hull

nudging its way between the bigger ships

just as her son had edged between older boys.

She has hatched a mesh of rigging,

– the working of the nail raising a blister at her finger's joint –

a firm and steady net of

taut lines, not

the adder-quick twist of a wet rope

to trip him, pitch him in –

the lines of her sketch show white

against the pillar's red

like the animal bones he brought home once,

sandbleached dry and white, or

like scars, gleaming in the raking light.

Rosemary Appleton

What is Evil Must Not be Forgotten

At first it had no name. It was not necessary. Men blessed the water, laid their dead at her side, but left her identity to the gods. Then, homesick perhaps, the first invaders named her 'Sequana', like the river where they had played as boys. New people came, laid roads, built bridges, and renamed her the Belisama. They too left, or stayed, forgot the old names and called their river Mersey. Many generations passed.

A man stands upon her bank.

"Eadgyth!"

His voice rings across the waters. He wades into the marsh but doesn't venture too far, afraid of how reeds mask the river's sudden depth. The strong, brown currents have taken more than one child.

"Eadgyth!"

"Patruus!"

He moves towards her, carries her, holding her precious weight against his chest but when his feet reach dry grass, he throws her and marches away. It is only later, when the moon has risen, that he is able to speak to her. His words float to the water and are carried away.

In London, a man dreams upon his palatial bed and hears the frightened father's talk of the river. When he wakes, the man, who is King, Lord, Duke and Count, yet wants more and fears less, decrees a Letters' Patent to a cluster of houses on the banks of the Mersey. From here great ships will sail, conquer new lands, and quell rebellion.

Centuries pass. Like a river fed by new tributaries, the original streets spawn lanes and alleys. New roads are built and majestic, hopeful buildings appear.

At the Canning Graving Docks, a man is looking to and fro, searching for something. Workmen pass, black with dirt. The stink of soldered iron pervades the air.

"William!" he shouts. "William!"

He climbs upon a crate in order to survey the dock.

Gladstone spots William and runs to him.

"Where were you?"

"I was in the hold of the ship." His eyes are shining. "People used to be laid side by side like spoons."

"Home!" Gladstone barks. "You will not walk with me again."

What is evil must not be forgotten. The songs of the slaves who jumped in leg irons, to the crack of sailors' whips, until their ankles were bleeding flesh, can still be heard today.

Yet the river, it is written, is a strong, brown god. Regardless it surges. A flood destroys yet if we wait, patiently, the waters will nourish the ground and bring forth a different future.

A man stands on the Albert Dock. It is dusk.

"Amy!" he shouts. He doesn't yet dare to look into the waters below.

"Daddy!"

He turns around and opens out his arms. The fireworks begin. An explosion of sound celebrates their reunion.

"What are those for, Daddy?" she asks.

"For us!" he says, swinging her in his arms.

"For Liverpool."

They look into the sky. Below them, beneath the thick iron rails, fireworks ripple on the surface of the river. The Mersey does not stop to reflect as she pushes her waters silently by.

Petra McQueen

North Sea, Redcar:
Mechanical Failure

More alive it seems than you, than me,
this place – such womb-notes fetched from deep,
its remembered pitch.

Across the front passenger seat
I reach out a hand
for your wound-down window, touch
instead the space of a heart,
that gentle *lub dub*,
something dark.

Michael Brown

When a Dock is Booming

"Even when a dock is booming there is something a little mysterious and forbidding about it and when it has passed its peak of prosperity there is something even more mysterious and forbidding about it. It's like an eye which once looked far out on to the world and from which the light had now dimmed."

from 'Gwyn Thomas visits Butetown'

"Not that I am biased," opined Max Boyce... But I am, having known the area in the late 1980s before the Cardiff Bay Barrage was built. I remember the old Butetown Police Station with a lamp post outside with an A4 picture of Lynette White on it. I had a printing business in an old warehouse and my window looked out at Butetown nick. My neighbour in Grangetown, 80 years young, remembers two policemen, big and tall coming in to the pubs at closing, one through the lounge door and one through the bar. One looking through at the other and having covered the room with their gaze, lifted the pint the landlord had pulled, and in one fell swoop drained it and out they went back through their respective doors to continue the two-step, four-step beat outside. Could have been The White Hart in James Street; it might have been The Packet at the bottom end of Bute Street. I'll slip into the vernacular for a moment and say: "You should really be 'aving a proper local writing this, a proper Cardiffian." But I'm doing it, a returner to the city that I lived in when man first stepped on the moon. We lived in Llandaff then, in 1969 when astronauts were manning the barricades and rioting on the streets of Europe. I returned in 1988 to live in Grangetown, less than two miles away but a world away really and only a mile away from that, was Butetown or 'The Docks' as we always called it because we would go drinking down there, to the pubs previously mentioned and to the Docks Non Political Club. The architecture of these buildings was/is massive. The old National Westminster Bank in Bute Street, the Coal Exchange Building which is now a hotel. You see I was only 23 and I didn't want to be running a printing business called Dinas Studios – I wanted to be out on the piss and that's what I did do in the end. The business was handed over to a partner who employed his son. Big new machines were installed instead of the piddly little sheet fed nightmare that I wiped with methyl ethyl ketone and kicked in my slumber as it failed and failed and failed. My neighbours told me later that they would laugh when they heard me kicking and swearing at the machine. They made stained glassed windows. They were proper artisans. There was a miserable man next door who fixed the old slot machines and fruit machines and he complained endlessly about the ink and the mess that I made in the communal sink with the rollers from the machine that I used to kick and kick.

Anybody who remembers the docks of the 1980s remembers the North Star where you would drink cans of Breaker and watch prostitutes dance with each other. No North Star no more, now the Norwegian Church has been moved, where I saw Vin Garbutt sing 'If I had a Son', written by Newport boy Phil Millichip, because I had asked him to do so, to sing, not write the song. It was about a man who didn't want his son to follow him down the pit. The Port of Cardiff was built on the back of coal. There is a statue of a miner in bronze pointing to the cliffs at Penarth where lies Joseph Parry who wrote 'Myfanwy'. Here now is Mermaid Quay, but I have never seen a mermaid down there, not even Shirley Bassey lookalikes in their hen party outfits. It's a mish mash I'm sorry to say, Cardiff Bay. It doesn't do it for this amateur psychogeographer who crosses the barrage by foot to get a glimpse of the Blue Bird Cranes. Not wildlife but dockside cranes still in use in the colours of Cardiff City Football Club. There is a strange statue to Captain Scott, frozen in mosaic. What really gets to me now – and I'll cut to the chase – is the artificiality of the place. I'm surprised they haven't put pink plastic garden flamingos down there. It offends one who remembers the gravitas, the character, the ebullience and the notoriety of the place. Now it has become a plasticine appendage to the plasticised city it serves.

"You can tells I'm not a proper Cardiffian likes cos I'm too critical of the place. I only wants it to be better see" (vernacular again, an 's' is added on to the end of whatever it can be). I remember a black guy from Butetown who did some work on my house saying that the day the docks changed was when cocaine came in. "It was chill with the cannabis but when they started dealing the Peruvian marching powder many peoples' heads started to go." That observation stayed with me because the new developments are like cocaine compared to the old ganja. New, bright and sharp, as opposed to old, slow and mellow. The pace of life went with the tide.

So the light gets in now but it is the artificial light used in supermarkets. It is the light reflecting off the 'art installation' outside the bright, shiny new Cardiff Bay Police Station. It is the light shining through the harbour lights of the Cardiff Bay Barrage. Iain Sinclair says that he can no longer write London. I would have to say the same for this particular part of Cardiff.

David Williams

A Place for Putting Out
or Pulling Up

*(At the Place for Pulling Up Boats – one word in Gaelic –
from 'Two Thieves' by Norman MacCaig)*

On the road to Killybegs a finger post points to Port

where the lane ends at a stony beach between

stacks and cliffs, fishing boats drawn up.

On the slope, ruins lie in rickles of bones

along a street, hearths and walls half-imagined.

Sailors from here knew each slavering rock by name,

every channel, every deceiving ledge.

They knew habits of tides and weathers.

Before reaching the open Atlantic

there's Toralaydan and Tormore Islands to pass,

Cnoc na Mara, Búd an Diabhal.

They put out crab pots, watched for shoals

climbed basalt stacks in search of eggs –

a lad was marooned for a month after weather turned

and starved to death. On the wind came smells

of turned earth and sea before the storms

of Famine hit. Those who survived it left the village,

only to find it everywhere. No records of the names.

Rebecca Gethin

A mile of straight single-track road lined with gorse. A golf course arcing along the low coastal edges of the narrow spit of land. A dormer bungalow. A lighthouse. An ice-cream van. A small car park that intermittently fills with coach-loads of day-tripping tourists – more than a hundred thousand every year. There, the recent addition of disabled parking, cycle stands and new seating. The sea is calm and blue round to Rosemarkie, but greyer, choppier round to Inverness. These, the changeable waters of the Black Isle and Moray Firth, across to the cannons of Fort George and the Highlanders Museum, and beyond to Nairn, Cromarty, Lossiemouth, Wilkhaven and Tarbat Ness. The small boats come in from Avoch, past Fortrose Harbour. On the shoreline, men with cameras and tripods gaze patiently. On the boats, people stand and point. They are waiting for the bottle-nosed dolphins, hoping they'll jump like salmon, hang in the air for a shutter-sweet second, before racing on, not ever knowing the meaning of 'port'.

About the authors

NICK ALLEN has recently twice been runner-up in international poetry competitions and was highly commended in the OWF Otley 'wildlife' competition. His first pamphlet, *The Necessary Line*, was published by Half Moon Books in October 2017. He talks to poets in darkened rooms at the back of pubs and sometimes feels enlightened.

ROSEMARY APPLETON is writer living in Suffolk, working in snatched moments, fuelled by coffee. She has had poems published in *Mslexia*, *Spontaneity*, *The Fenland Reed* and in anthologies by PaperSwans Press and Eyewear.

MATEI BEJENARU is an artist and founder of the Periferic Biennial in Iași, Romania. He examines the politics of representation in documentary photography and film and methods of generation of hybrid art projects at the confluence between visual arts, poetry, experimental music and scientific research. He teaches photography and video at George Enescu National University of the Arts, Iaşi.

TESSA BERRING is a writer and artist based in Edinburgh. Her writing can be found in a variety of magazines/anthologies, etc. with new work forthcoming via *Mote*, *Tentacular Magazine* and *Tenebræ*. She is a member of '12', a writers' collective based mostly in Scotland, but also Nottingham.

MW BEWICK grew up on the edge of the Lake District and now lives in Essex. He is co-founder and editor at Dunlin Press, and teaches creative writing at London College of Creative Media. His poems have appeared in journals including *Under The Radar*, *The Stinging Fly*, and *Envoi*, plus a number of anthologies. With Dunlin Press he has published a first collection of poetry, *Scarecrow* (2017), and a collaboration with Ella Johnston, *The Orphaned Spaces* (2018), on the subject of edgelands and brownfield sites.

MICHAEL BROWN'S work has been published widely in magazines including *The Rialto*, *Southword*, *The North* and many others. In 2015 he was shortlisted for the Bare Fiction Collection was placed third in the York Poetry Prize. He was selected by Clare Pollard for a Northern Writers' Award (New North Poets) in 2017. He has twice been shortlisted in the Basil Bunting Award, and in 2018 he won the Wirral Firsts Poetry Competition and was commended in the McLellan Prize. His first pamphlet, *Undersong* (2014) is available from Eyewear. *Locations for a Soul* (2016) was published by Templar. His debut full-length collection, in which 'North Sea, Redcar: Mechanical Failure' first appears, was published by Salt in 2019.

ALISON CAMPBELL is from Aberdeen and now lives in London. She is a teacher/counsellor And has had poems in various publications, including *Obsessed with Pipework* and *The Curlew*. She was shortlisted for the Segora Poetry Prize (2018) and was commended in the Barnet Poetry competition in 2017 and 2018.

VAHNI CAPILDEO is a writer based in Edinburgh and Trinidad, West Indies. She won the Forward Prize for poetry for *Measures of Expatriation* (Carcanet, 2016). Other collections include *Venus as a Bear* (Carcanet, 2018) and *Skin Can Hold* (Carcanet, 2019), and she has also created texts for installation and theatre, including reworkings of Old Norse literature.

SARAH-CLARE CONLON is a copywriter and proofreader, and literature editor of *Creative Tourist*. The inaugural writer-in-residence at Manchester's 'water palace' Victoria Baths, her creative writing has been published by Centre for New Writing, Comma, Dostoyevsky Wannabe, Flash, Reflex Fiction, Salt, Spelk, Stand and The Other Room, and in upcoming Arachne anthology *Story Cities*. She co-skippered a small yacht, *Hedhyu*, around the Irish Sea in 2007.

TIM COOKE is a teacher, freelance journalist and creative writing PhD student. He has written about film, literature, place and education for various publications, including the *Guardian*, *Little White Lies*, *New Welsh Review*, *3AM* magazine, the *Quietus*, *Ernest Journal*, *EYE* and the *Hackney Citizen*, among others. His creative work has appeared in *Black Static*, *Prole*, *The Shadow Booth*, *Lune*, *The Nightwatchman*, *Elsewhere*, *Lampeter Review*, *Drain*, *Foxhole*, *Porridge*, *Stepz*, *Storgy*, *Particulations*, *Glove*, *Litro* and MIR Online. He recently won Adventures in Fiction's New Voices Award for his current project *The Town*. You can follow him on Twitter: @cooketim2

DR SETH CROOK has taught philosophy at various universities, is transitioning into a seal, and lives on Mull. His poems have most recently appeared in such places as *The Rialto*, *Magma*, *Envoi*, *The Interpreter's House*, *Northwords Now*, *Southlight*, *The Nitrogen House*, the *Glasgow Review of Books*.

MOIRA GARLAND has migrated from ports of call, Liverpool and Hong Kong, to the inland city of Leeds. Her poetry publications include *The North, One for the Road* (Smith/Doorstop), *Algebra of Owls, Until the Stars Burn Out, Mythologies* (Indigo Dreams), and *Watch the Birdie*. Her poems have won, or been commended, in competitions. @moiragauthor

REBECCA GETHIN had two pamphlets published in 2017. She has been a Hawthornden Fellow and undertook a residency at Brisons Veor. Messages was a winner in the Coast to Coast to Coast pamphlet competition (2018), and *Vanishings* is forthcoming from Palewell Press.

CAROLINE GILL was awarded third prize in the Milestones Poetry Competition (2017), judged by Brian Patten and organised by Write Out Loud. She was overall winner of the inaugural ZSL Poetry Competition on the theme of conservation (2014). Her commissioned chapbook *The Holy Place*, co-authored with John Dotson, was published in 2012 by Peter Thabit Jones of The Seventh Quarry (Wales), in conjunction with Stanley H Barkan of Cross-Cultural Communications (New York). Caroline's poems have been published in the UK, USA, Australia, Romania, India and Italy. Caroline is married to archaeologist, David Gill, and is an active member of Suffolk Poetry Society. Website: carolinegillpoetry.com

JASON GOULD is a creative writing graduate from the University of Hull. His short fiction has been published in various anthologies and magazines, for which he has gained a number of honourable mentions. In addition, he is a British Fantasy Society Award shortlistee. His academic paper on the nature of evil in science fiction is published by Luna Press (2019).

FEE GRIFFIN is an MA creative writing student at the University of Lincoln, as well as being a cleaner and working in a pub. Her two main writing interests are poetry and life writing that includes a fictional element. Griffin is particularly interested in work that intersects genres.

JANET HATHERLEY lives in London and is a special needs teacher. Her poems have been published in magazines including *Artemis, The Curlew, The Interpreter's House, Under the Radar* and *Coast to Coast to Coast*. She won third prize in the Barnet competition (2015), was commended in Cannon Poets Sonnet or Not (2017), Ware and Ver Poets competitions (2018), and had poems longlisted for the Segora competition (2018). She has had two pamphlets shortlisted for Coast to Coast to Coast and has a poem in the *Play* anthology by Susan Taylor and Simon Williams (2018).

JULIE HOGG is published in many literary journals including *Abridged, Black Light Engine Room, Butcher's Dog, Corrugated Wave, Honest Ulsterman, Irisi, Poethead, Poetry Bus Mag, Proletarian Poetry, Well Versed* and *Words for the Wild*. Featured in anthologies by Ek Zuban, Litmus, Zoomorphic and Seren, her debut pamphlet *Majuba Road* is available from Vane Women Press.

SARAH JASMON is a novelist and creative writing lecturer at Manchester Met. She spends half of her time living on a boat on the Leeds/Liverpool canal, and the other half in Manchester, where she is working on a PhD looking at the place of the Manchester canals in the life and story of the city. Her research is a creative/critical mix, combining elements of place writing, psychogeography and cultural history, questioning why the canals are left out of much of Manchester's narrative.

RG JODAH lives in London, enjoying metropolitan anonymity. Recent works have been published in the *Lampeter Review, Typishly, Dream Catcher, Southlight, Lighten Up Online, London Grip* and *Three Drops from a Cauldron*.

ELLA JOHNSTON is an artist, illustrator and journalist. Her drawings and paintings explore time, memory and human connections/encounters with place, particularly the natural world. Ella was born in London and lives in Wivenhoe, Essex. She is a co-founder, art director and editor at Dunlin Press.

CHARLIE LAMBERT is a former sports broadcaster who began writing poetry in 2016. His work has appeared in the human rights anthology *Write to be Counted* (The Book Mill, 2017) and also in *This Place I Know* (Handstand Press, 2018), as well as multiple publications on the news-oriented website Poetry24.co.uk. He is a member of the Liverpool Dead Good Poets Society and lives in Liverpool.

GARY LIGGETT is an English film-maker, writer and poet. He was born near the banks of the River Mersey, from where he once sailed to the Isle of Man in a boat built with his father. His work is held in permanent collections, including the Museum of Modern Art in New York and the Wordsworth Trust, England. He lives sustainably on a Cumbrian smallholding with his wife and family.

CHRIS MAILLARD is a wordsmith for hire, for pleasure and for lack of other options. Also uncomplicated cook, deeply average guitarist, vaguely competent bicycle builder, occasionally successful gardener, secret graphic designer, emergency photographic assistant, parent, peasant, pest. He hangs his mildly Dylanesque hat in the East of London and the South of Norfolk.

JESSICA MAYHEW is the author of two pamphlets, *Someone Else's Photograph* (Crystal Clear Creators, 2012) and *Amok* (Eyewear, 2015). Her poetry, short stories and essays have been published in journals such as *Ambit, Stand, Magma* and *The Interdisciplinary Literary Studies Journal.* Jessica has given readings at Lyric Lounge Northampton, the Leicester Shindig, and Smack the Poesy. She has also read from her pamphlets at the Nottingham and Ledbury poetry festivals, as well as in London.

BETH MCDONOUGH trained in silversmithing at Glasgow School of Art. Following an M.Litt at Dundee University, she was writer in residence at Dundee Contemporary Arts (2014-16). Her work is strongly connected to place, particularly to the Tay, where she swims, and forages nearby. Her poetry may be read in *Gutter,*

Stand, *Agenda*, *Poetry Salzburg Review* and many other journals and anthologies. She reviews at DURA. *Handfast* (Mother's Milk Books, 2016), a poetry duet pamphlet with Ruth Aylett, is a verse investigation of her experience of her son's autism, as her co-poet considers that of her parents' dementia. Her own first pamphlet will be published later this year.

PETRA MCQUEEN is a writer and teacher. Her writing has appeared in the *Saturday Evening Post*, the *Guardian*, and *You* magazine, among many other publications. She has won several prizes for her prose, including first prize in the National Association of Writers' Groups' Short Story Competition. She lives close to the mudflats of northeast Essex, with her large, lively family. She runs her own writing workshops (thewriterscompany.co.uk), has taught creative writing at Essex University, and is currently working on a novel.

MARTIN NEWELL is an English writer, poet and rock musician. He founded the band Cleaners from Venus and has recorded many albums under this name as well under his own. He has written for the *Independent*, the *Independent on Sunday*, the *Sunday Express*, the *Guardian* and the *East Anglian Daily Times*. As well as a dozen poetry collections, Newell has published a number of books including two instalments of his rock memoir, *This Little Ziggy* and *The Greatest Living Englishman*.

KERRI NÍ DOCHARTAIGH lives in northwest Ireland. She writes about nature, literature and place for publications which include *The Clearing*, *Oh Comely* magazine, *New Welsh Review*, *Caught by the River* and *The London Magazine*. She is learning to speak Irish and exploring her folkloric island in a Transit Van.

DR GOLNOOSH NOUR is the author the poetry collection *Sorrows of the Sun* which was published in 2017 under her pseudonym Sogol Sur. She has performed both her prose and poetry in numerous literary events across the UK. In 2019 she completed a PhD in literature and creative writing, and she teaches prose and poetry at Birkbeck and the University of East London.

MARK RANGER is an autism practitioner and environmental writer working in Hampshire and West Sussex. Through his PhD research he is seeking to formalise an aesthetic theory of exclosure. These overlooked and untidy spaces appear in this work on ports, which contributes, alongside his other writing, towards a radically ethical way of interpreting landscape.

ELIZABETH LEE REYNOLDS is a writer and activist who primarily focuses on themes of environmental politics and place. She has an MA in wild writing from the University of Essex and has been published in a number of places, including the Dunlin Press anthology *The Migrant Waders* and pieces in *The Ecologist*. She is interested in the power of communities for environmental and social good, as well as debunking green consumerism.

DR ANNA SERGI holds a PhD in sociology from the University of Essex. Her specialism is in organised crime studies and comparative criminal justice. She has published extensively in renowned peer-review journals in criminology on topics related to Italian mafias both in Italy and abroad, as well as on policing strategies against organised crime across states.

BRYAN THOMAS an amateur poet and writer of biography and fiction (mostly short stories), having retired from his own self-employed architectural practice in northeast Essex. Married with four children (and four steps!) he has lived in Wivenhoe, Essex, or thereabouts, almost long enough to become a 'local'.

ALEX TOMS is a repeat winner in national poetry competitions and in 2015 was Manchester Cathedral Poet of the Year. She is widely published in magazines, journals and anthologies. Her debut collection *Lessons for an Apprentice Eel Catcher* was published by Dunlin Press in 2018.

LYDIA UNSWORTH is the author of two collections of poetry: *Certain Manoeuvres* (Knives Forks & Spoons, 2018) and *Nostalgia for Bodies* (Erbacce, 2018), for which she won the 2018 Erbacce Poetry Prize. Her work can be found in *Ambit, Pank, Litro, Tears in the Fence, Banshee, Ink Sweat and Tears*, and others. She is based in Manchester/Amsterdam. Twitter: @lydiowanie

ROB WALTON is a writer, performer and teacher from Scunthorpe, who now lives in Whitley Bay. He writes poetry, short stories and flash fictions for adults and children. His work appears in a variety of magazines and anthologies. He has also written script and collated the text for the New Hartley Memorial Pathway. He sometimes tweets: @anicelad

DAVID WILLIAMS is a blogger and psychogeographer. He lives in Cardiff and writes clenched fist poetry and crime fiction. He is the creator of Ken Frane: last of the Cardiff Docks' detectives.

Also from Dunlin Press

Est: Collected Reports From East Anglia
A journey through the landscapes of East Anglia, *Est* is a unique collection of prose, poetry and reportage that spans the Wash to the Thames and the Fens to the German Sea. The texts merge psychogeography, social history, personal memoir and travel writing with discourses on local fable, art, archaeology and conservation.

The Migrant Waders
A collection of evocative prose, poetry and reportage that follows the migration routes of wading and shore birds from the high arctic to the tropics. Taking in the histories of the people and places where the birds make their temporary homes, the book includes 21 avian illustrations.

Scarecrow, MW Bewick
This debut poetry collection from MW Bewick transfigures contemporary landscapes of the city and the countryside in an unsettling flux of fractured narrative time and atomised human agency. This thought-provoking volume brings together registers of folk, baroque and the surreal to confront a 21st-century sense of existential crisis.

Priced Out, Tinsel Edwards
A powerful look at the declining state of housing in the capital through the eyes of an artist. Edwards traces the high rises in cost of accommodation, spiralling property prices, and skewers the reasons why artists, who, like many others, contribute so much to the character and uniqueness of London life, are being priced out of the city.

The Orphaned Spaces, MW Bewick and Ella Johnston
An illustrated exploration of overlooked areas of natural beauty – edgelands, ex-industrial, derelict and brownfield sites, and the sometimes rare flora and fauna that is found there. More than a nature book, it is a rumination on life, loss and time, through the prism of liminal spaces.

Lessons for an Apprentice Eel Catcher, Alex Toms
In her debut collection of poems, Toms introduces us to a troupe of curious characters to explore themes of love, womanhood and sex. Her poems skilfully summon the uncanny, and out of it draws a slithering sense with which we are all familiar.

dunlinpress.com